SIX CAR LENGTHS
BEHIND AN ELEPHANT

UNDERCOVER & OVERWHELMED
AS A CIA WIFE AND MOTHER

SIX CAR LENGTHS
BEHIND AN ELEPHANT

UNDERCOVER & OVERWHELMED
AS A CIA WIFE AND MOTHER

Lillian McCloy

 Bordertown
Publishing
Berkeley, California

Bordertown Publishing
Berkeley, CA

www.bordertownpublishing.com

Edited by Johanna McCloy
Copyedited by Mary DeDanan
Cover Design by Teddi Black
Formatted by Johanna McCloy and Teddi Black

Six Car Lengths Behind an Elephant: Undercover & Overwhelmed as a CIA Wife and Mother by Lillian McCloy—First Edition.

ISBN 978-0-9975963-0-4

Author's Note

This is the story of my nomadic life as the wife of a man who worked under deep cover for the CIA. This is not an expose of the CIA. It is a story about how I endured as both wife and mother, living under great pressure and in strange lands.

Everything written in this narrative is true. However, it was necessary that I exercise extreme discretion in revealing details that might disclose the identity of the American companies who so valiantly agreed to hire my husband. They trusted that he would do his job well while also allowing him the freedom he required to accomplish what was necessary for his true vocation. Because of this, I have reluctantly excluded some details that might have contributed more vivid descriptions of people and places and activities, and which would have made the story more complete. Most of the names have been changed to protect the innocent and the sly.

My admiration and respect for the American institutions who showed their confidence in my husband, and who consistently displayed their faith in him without question, by far exceeds the need to embroider a book. These people were true patriots who took enormous risks. We were at all times grateful to them.

Contents

"They arrive at a point in life having themselves, in their demanding and dominating (false) selves, lived a lie—where they mistrust almost everyone, look for the hidden meaning and motives behind even the most sincere statements of friends and loved ones."

—Winston McKinley Scott, CIA Deep Cover Officer, Mexico

"When you play on the street, it's part of the game. I know that. Just don't ask me to like it."

—Tess Trueheart to Dick Tracy

Training (1962-1964)

No Need to Know

"I've applied for a job with the CIA!" Frank revealed over the phone with excitement. "I took a number of tests today, and I have a psychiatric test tomorrow."

I couldn't take this seriously. Frank had just earned his master's degree in political science and international relations, graduating at the top of his class. In our discussions about the career avenues he might consider, where his particular skills would be most pertinent, we agreed that there had to be a branch of the government seeking someone with his background. He had consequently gone to Washington to apply for a job with the Foreign Service. One of the men conducting interviews had perused Frank's résumé and thought he was a likely candidate for the CIA. Frank knew the CIA housed numerous departments and was immediately taken with the thought of being involved in one of them. I had no inkling that this news might be something I shouldn't talk about. I assumed he might work in an office job as a staff member in Washington. Being a spy was too ludicrous a notion and, as a matter of fact, did not even occur to me.

When Frank called with his news, I was having coffee with my friend Christine. We were both pregnant at the time, she with her first child and I with our second. She had been asking me what to expect when labor started and I told her that "you'll probably have false labor pains," because I was experiencing them myself. I was seven months into my pregnancy. Frank and I had agreed it was a safe time for him to be away and leave me on my own with our son John.

That same night, I had a dream so startling and frightening that it woke me up. I turned on the light and was horrified to discover that I was hemorrhaging. Afraid to move, my first thought was that I had to call my neighbor, Mary, who was not only a good friend but also a nurse. I had telephoned her only once before, because we were so accustomed to seeing each other daily, but on that one occasion, she had guests, so I had looked up her number in the phone book. Amazingly, I remembered and dialed the correct number, and Mary immediately came over and wrapped me in bath towels while her husband called the hospital and brought his car up front.

I was so weak that I had to lie down in the back seat. "Guess what?" I said as the car began to roll. "Looks like Frank has a job with the CIA." I was going into shock, not recognizing the severity of my condition. I was shaking when we arrived at the hospital at four in the morning, and my doctor was waiting at the door with what appeared to be the entire hospital staff on alert. As I was put on a gurney and rushed to the room with the doctor beside me, I cheerfully said, "Did you know that my husband has a job with the CIA?" "That's nice," he said in a tone used to speak to children, as we tore down the hall. After being hooked up to equipment used for blood transfusions, I felt compelled to tell the nurse as well.

I was in full labor now, ho hum, and shaking with cold and good cheer. My doctor came in and told me there was no time to waste if he was going to save my life because my blood pressure had dropped dangerously. I had never seen him so stern. He said he had to perform a cesarean and that it would possibly sacrifice the life of my child. I said, "No, no, no, that's absurd. Take me to the delivery room and I'll be fine." Without my permission, or Frank's, he could not operate. He threw his hands with an I-give-up gesture, and I found myself hurtling down the corridor to the delivery room. "Guess what?" I told the orderly. "My husband works for the CIA!"

And Kristin was born. She was five pounds of perfect baby with a sweep of dark eyelashes. The nurses exclaimed at her beauty, and the doctor did an Irish jig. I was in a very good mood. Kristin was rushed to an incubator and I was put in a room, with transfusions dripping into both arms. My dear doctor came in, still in his scrubs, mask hanging under his chin. "God," he said shaking his head, "you scared me." He sat down with his hands on his knees, head bowed. "By the way," I said, "did I tell you Frank is going to be working for the CIA?"

Frank's cover was blown before he was hired.

At that time, I had never heard of the unbendable creed: "No Need To Know."

Frank

Everything in Frank's background had a common thread. It seemed to me that he had been courting danger from the time he was released from the confines of the family home. He had not been allowed to ride a bicycle until he was twelve years old (although at fourteen he was secretly learning to drive a car). His parents had coddled him to save him from the danger in the street and the danger in the world. When he was a child, if he had a head cold he was bundled up and taken to the doctor or even to the emergency room at the hospital. He was born late in his parents' life and they treasured him. Their fears became an integral part of his life: Be careful. Don't cross the street. Watch for cars. Don't climb so high.

He was raised a Catholic, attending Catholic schools. His parents dreamed that he'd become a priest and when he was an altar boy, he seriously pondered it. When he reached his teens, he knew he could not make the sacrifice, but he continued to say the rosary twice a day. In some cases, the fears of the parents are foisted on the child, but in Frank's case, he was eager to break away, to take risks, and to experience what had hitherto been forbidden thrills.

Frank wanted to drive fast cars, buy an ocelot for a pet, and kiss a girl (in that order). Even kissing a girl appeared to be a dangerous experiment. He had a crush on the girl next door, a daughter of family friends, but was clandestinely watched by his father, who wanted to ensure that there would be nothing to confess to a priest. When Frank and the girl sat on a swing on the front porch, his father watched from the shadows of the street.

There was so much for Frank to rebel against. His new job covered all the bases.

Frank would have been the perfect selection for the college debating team. He was literary, articulate and witty, a voracious reader and a consummate politician in the truest sense of the word. But that was not macho enough. As an extracurricular activity, he chose boxing. When describing his first boxing match, Frank said his opponent looked like Bruno, the menacing and fearsome brute in the comic strip *Popeye*. Within three minutes, Frank found himself back in the locker room with a concussion. It was the beginning and end of his boxing career.

After graduating from college, Frank told his parents that he was going to join the Marine Corps and become a fighter pilot. His mother fell apart, begging him to reconsider, as I certainly would have done if our son had proposed such a move. It was a stunning decision for a college graduate with straight As and the entire world at his feet. There were multiple choices he could've explored, but he was adamant.

Having obtained his degree in political science and international relations, joining the CIA under deep cover fit into his pattern. Upon being accepted, he was told that he could tell only one member of his family, and he chose his sister. I, too, told my sister. I didn't believe that there was a reality behind the plots of books and movies about spies, and I had never been interested in those books, but our parents would have been bewildered and frightened.

It was probably Frank's political bent that best suited him to the world of espionage, his ability to juggle wit and wisdom and manipulate the minds of others. This was the true talent that deep cover required. It was all about people, not about guns and fast cars, and it was also sufficiently dangerous to appeal to him.

Although he couldn't resist the experience of paramilitary training, he did not earn high grades there. His strong suit was not body coordination, but he did run with the tough guys and again proved he could compete. He had to prove to the world that he was not a sissy, a description he had been branded with as a boy. He was courtly and courageous and clever, and his eyes danced when he called a bluff.

He came to love his work. It didn't matter how much he hated the bean counters. His love for his job overshadowed the dogma of the guys with the green eyeshades.

When Frank had talked about his dream of having a job that involved travel, I assumed he meant travel for *him*, as I certainly had no wanderlust. It was a miracle that I had dragged my earthbound cleats out of the Canadian mud to make the move to San Francisco, a move fueled by my infatuation with the city and the pain of a doomed relationship I left behind.

Neither of us thought that this trip to Washington would mean anything more than a good place to start. When the exotic CIA beckoned, Frank was elated. He couldn't believe his good luck. He'd been a fighter pilot in the Marine Corps and now he found, to his delight, another job that could scare him to death.

Having just squeezed through several months of knuckle-whitening financial straits, collecting five cents for each empty Coca-Cola bottle, while Frank earned his master's degree on the GI Bill, even the most mundane job with a decent salary was attractive, and for Frank, a job in Washington was very exciting indeed.

San Francisco to D.C.

My love affair with San Francisco was almost visceral. After one visit, I had been completely beguiled by the beauty of that city and with great good luck I had found an excellent job in the heart of it and an apartment on a hill with a view. Moving away meant leaving all of that.

Our worldly possessions were paltry. I made the mistake of doing all the packing, and this mistake became the pattern in future years, when the packing procedure was a monumental task, even when carried out by professionals. The master of the house was inevitably deeply involved in training for his new job in another country, or leaving town for briefing and orientation, while I organized and orchestrated the lives of our children, the madness of passports, visas, schools, and good-byes, the latter always the most difficult. After having met American women in foreign countries, I found that this was the norm.

We arrived in Washington on a cold and rainy November night. It was the kind of rain that boded sleet or snow. We did not disembark from the plane directly into a warm airport. We scuttled down a small flight of stairs onto the tarmac and clumsily ran to the shelter of the airport building.

Someone from the Agency was to meet us at the airport. This person was to transport us to our temporary lodging and then help and advise us during the oncoming weeks. It was an enormous relief to be met by a married couple who were veterans of the CIA. Their warm welcome made it clear that this was more than a job they had to do. When the woman reached out to take the baby from my arms and then put her other arm around me, I had a good feeling about the kind of support we could expect in the future. Although we were escorted to a dark, little, furnished apartment in a compound of many dark, furnished apartments, our mentors inspired us to think positively.

We had no winter clothes, and at that time, no car. There was a drug store within walking distance, but no sign of any other commercial stores. Frank was picked up to be briefed on the following snowy morning, and when he closed the door behind him, I looked around at the gloomy living room, already festooned with drying diapers on the backs of chairs. I felt a wash of misgivings envelop me. How was I expected to keep house here without access to a supermarket, without a car, and without warm clothes? How long were we expected to stay here? What had we done? Our future was upon us on a daily basis, and the rest was a mystery.

When Mrs. "Mentor" arrived at our front door, I threw my arms around her, and she returned the embrace as well as she could, considering she was carrying bags of groceries. "This should get you started," she said, "but tonight you will have dinner at our house." That night, when we were introduced to their noisy brood of children and sat in front of a blazing fire, my spirits picked up. This was the future, I hoped.

Frank seemed to take the ensuing days in stride. He was interested in the "job" but so far, it was no job at all; he was merely sitting at a desk in an office in downtown Washington, from nine to five. A week after our arrival, Frank sat on the bed, holding his chest, and said he felt like he was having a heart attack. This, I thought, was the only indication that he was apprehensive about the path we were on. He had shown no sign of doubt before. I believed that the pain he felt was probably a pulled muscle caused by carrying heavy luggage, and that what he needed was a heating pad. The drug store! I put on sneakers and two pairs of socks and waded through the snow to buy him a heating pad, and as I lumbered home, I thought longingly of my bachelor apartment on a hill in San Francisco, my office with my name on a brass plaque on the door, and my salary, which had been higher than Frank's.

I was filled with foreboding. Why had I agreed to this choice? In the months that followed, we were to learn that our dark little apartment was, in the parlance of the CIA, a "safe house." We had no idea that we were dangerous.

The Face of the CIA

Although the Old School Tie theory is true of the CIA, any applicant had to pass extremely difficult tests to be accepted. Being with the CIA was "classy." Part of the reason for that was that it was largely made up of graduates from Harvard, Princeton, and Yale, and it followed that the rather snobbish esteem with which the CIA was purportedly viewed appealed to the new grads from Ivy League schools.

This might explain why members of the State Department later seemed to look upon the CIA with disdain. I guess we were the "rich kids." At first, Frank and I found this puzzling. Were we looked upon as "the elite" of the diplomatic corps? Were we supposed to think we were? Certainly this was an image that did not emanate from us. Nevertheless, the CIA was separate from the State Department and that left an air of mystery, which might have appeared as special privileges, whatever they were.

Those in the CIA who chose to work within the U.S. Embassy were under the umbrella of the political section. Over the years, in different countries, we came to realize that these individuals not only enjoyed the safety of diplomatic immunity, they were also far more likely to be promoted on a regular basis. They enjoyed the luxury of the commissary and the PX in almost any country, with their bounty of American products. They were also provided with housing, usually in an apartment complex owned by the embassy, which was not always a blessing, as we on our own could rent houses. In essence, they were not necessarily exposed to culture shock the same way we were, as they lived in a small piece of America.

True, we had a selection of where we could live, but there was a limit to the rent allowed, and the search for housing could be taxing. We did enjoy the bonus of receiving all the perks given by our cover company, such as a car and driver, as well as the occasional American club membership, depending on the company. There were times, however, when I would have been happy to have the safety and the sense of roots that government housing provided overseas. Not to mention, the feeling of family that those people must have experienced with all their neighbors, who also worked in the embassy and could be instant sources of advice and camaraderie. What we envied most was their private medical card, which was most important in third world countries.

We, on the outside, were dropped into place with nobody to guide us, unless we were lucky enough to have some time with the man Frank was replacing, if there was anyone in that position. The Old School Tie was little comfort to us when we found ourselves totally alone.

CIA employees like Frank are called case officers. Unlike common parlance, "agents" are actually the people who case officers recruit to do the spying for them. CIA case officers who work with the embassy are referred to as being "on the inside." In the course of this story, whenever the term "liaison with the embassy" or "representative of the embassy" is used, it is a reference to a member of CIA's personnel, and not to the embassy in general.

In some cases, the other case officer with whom my husband worked was in charge of all operations. In the countries where there was a very large contingent of the CIA, the case officer reported to a more senior intelligence officer who was "the boss."

What is Deep Cover?

Deep cover officers are responsible to the cover company to do the actual job and to do it well. It is not a pretending game. When Frank was assigned to a company as vice president of sales, it was his responsibility to train for the job in a very short period of time, and to succeed in that position. Only the president of the company and Frank's immediate superior were informed of his other, very real job. Of course, this meant that the entire staff in his office should have no doubt about his qualifications.

Most of his clandestine meetings took place in the evenings, usually in hotel rooms, often requiring an overnight stay to avoid suspicion. Men under deep cover had to expect to work twelve hours a day or more, and were expected to travel on company business whenever it seemed feasible. It demanded a lot of time away from the family.

Frank had several passports from various countries, each one used for a particular hotel, thereby appearing to be an authentic businessman and a regular guest. In foreign countries it was necessary to show one's passport at the hotel registry, so keeping a low profile was of paramount importance.

The double life was a juggling act and I was the juggler. When I got up at 6:30 a.m. to wake the children and make breakfast, I always closed our bedroom door because Daddy was "still sleeping," when in fact, he had not been home at all. Occasionally, the story was that he was out of town on a buying trip.

Lying to the children was very hard, especially when they were teenagers. The duplicity becomes a part of you and the lying is constant. Lying to your friends, your neighbors, your office staff, and your family becomes so natural that the lie becomes the truth in your mind, a part of who you are. At times the guilt was heavy, but for the most part the deceit was automatic. In hindsight, I am ashamed of how easy it was. It was an enormous betrayal. We confided only in each other, which, oddly enough, resulted in an even stronger bond between us.

Deep cover in the CIA means, literally, that you are so buried in the files of the Agency that your real name never appears anywhere, not even on the payroll. It means that you will have no contact with your embassy in a foreign country unless a message must be conveyed, and this is done in the most clandestine way, usually at their behest, with the understanding that under no circumstance will the embassy acknowledge or help you. Don't bother to call.

My husband agreed to live this life primarily because of the zeal we felt about President Kennedy. Frank wanted to be a part of his new America. It was also a chance for Frank to play cops and robbers all his life. Run around the corner and don't get caught. Dress up in odd clothes to walk through an airport, or register at a hotel, presenting your fake passport at the front desk, a passport bearing your picture, which matches your mustache and heavy glasses, and verifies that you are indeed a German businessman.

There is no question in my mind that CIA agents love their job because it is dangerous. Danger is fun. Consider that the first thing an infant will laugh at is peek-a-boo, or just boo! Later, it is hide-and-seek, looking for something hiding behind the curtains, or under the stairs. Graduate to a rollercoaster. The adrenaline pours, the heart pounds. Even a stolen kiss behind a kitchen door is delicious because it carries the possibility of getting caught. Flying a jet fighter in combat . . . the rush . . . the speed . . . the possibility of having to eject, like being shot out of a cannon, tearing through the sky alone. Free falling, parachute jumping . . . All these things are thrilling, because they are scary. Looking into a store window to study your reflection, eyes darting to see if anyone is behind you. Standing at the registration desk of a hotel, hiding in the body of someone who does not exist . . . will anyone recognize you?

The fun never ends. There are no guns. There are no tuxedos. No private plane flown over the mountains. There is no "Bond. James Bond," because he would never utter his name, far less be famous. And "spy" is a word that is never used, except in jest. Under deep cover there is nobody to turn to for help. If you are arrested, you will go to jail. Your name appears nowhere and you have become nobody.

You are out in the cold.

Always.

The Farm

The place where all CIA intelligence officers were trained was whimsically called "the Farm." It was reputed to be a military base, staffed with stern young soldiers who were visible at the gate and patrolling the grounds. Only those families who had small children qualified for housing on the base. It was a little like tract housing and had a feeling of neighborhood, albeit a neighborhood comprised mostly of women and children. The men attended classes in a barracks-like compound (where the bachelors lived), taught by instructors who were not much older than they were, but who had experience in the field. We learned that in most cases, they had blown their cover in a foreign country or had been removed from a post because it had grown potentially dangerous for their particular situation. This was a "cooling off" period. They taught the craft of intelligence gathering and explained the web in which it was woven.

There was another aspect of their itinerary, which was more physical and more fun, such as how to make plastic explosives and apply them to the underbellies of cars, then actually blow them up. There, in an open field were several used cars to destroy. Nobody knew where they came from, but they all knew that our own cars didn't look that good. There was a rush of passionate pleas to blow up our own cars, and let us have one of the cars in the field, but the pleas were ignored. Apparently they were accustomed to the request, but I suppose it was unethical to agree. (Unethical?) There was no explanation as to where the cars came from, but Frank surmised that they were repossessed from delinquent owners. We continued to drive our ancient, rattling Ford. In the course of Frank's career, there was never an occasion to blow up a car, and, in reminiscing, we wondered if anybody ever did.

Another break from the notebooks was parachute training, initially practiced from what I called a very tall tree house, for lack of a better description. It was a stand built somewhat like a guard's lookout, and from a stand on the top, they jumped into a very large pile of hay. Of course, there was no way to imitate the real jump. On one clear afternoon, "all systems were go" and they bounded on to the plane. Frank, beaming excitedly, explained where I could stand to see them in the distance, but I declined.

Security at the Farm was tight. The guardhouse at the entrance was the barrier through which any visitors must pass, displaying an ID with a picture, which was issued at the Farm itself. Military guards constantly patrolled our streets twenty-four hours a day. I found this comforting, as the women spent most evenings alone. There were certain areas we could not enter, or even ask about. These areas were indicated by large, threatening signs, and guarded by soldiers with guns. We could hear the sounds of their activities, the shouting of men, the shooting of guns, muffled explosions. Once, when I was driving through the maze of small dirt roads within the camp, I took a wrong turn and got lost. (I was a terrifying driver, too. The neighbors clutched their children when I pulled out of the driveway). My two toddlers were in the back seat. I stopped to get my bearings. The moment I stopped, a very young soldier loomed from behind rocks and shrubs and said, wearily, "Mrs. McCloy, I should have shot you. Go home." He knew my name, which I thought was very nice. They were serious about their warnings.

Later, Frank told me they were training guerrillas to be sent to Vietnam, and the guerrillas were Vietnamese.

If we wanted to leave the base for grocery shopping, we car-pooled, stopping at the guardhouse to explain our expedition and present IDs. Even our telephone calls were monitored. If any of us wanted to make a long distance call, it had to go through an operator who would ask who we wanted to call and why, then explain it to an officer and give permission. We assumed the calls were bugged. After having gone through the most intense scrutiny of our lives to be accepted by the CIA, I wondered what diabolical plans they could have expected of us, if we were silly enough to make these plans by telephone and from the base. We had been warned not to tell our families of our location. There was a post office box in the nearby town for us to receive mail, which was picked up by a guard. Did this make any sense? We were in limbo for several months. "Dear Mom: We are in limbo. Don't ask."

While at the Farm, there was little done for the wives to prepare for their future. Someone decided that language lessons would be helpful. Even though not everyone would be destined to use the language chosen, Spanish seemed to be the most likely to be used, as Spain, Mexico, and all of South America could become our destiny. A Spanish tutor came to one of our houses, and though I thought it might be a useless endeavor, it was a learning experience. On the morning of our first lesson, I didn't attend because I had laryngitis. My voice was nothing but a whisper, and extremely husky. I crossed the street to tell my neighbor, because I couldn't talk loud enough to be heard over the phone. She and I had arranged to go together to the lesson, children in tow. Her two sons and John liked to play together.

A short while after returning home, I wondered where John was. We didn't worry too much about the children, because our

Marines were always patrolling, and would instantly notice a lost child. Had John gone along to the class with my neighbor?

There was an area across from our house that was a tangle of brush and shrubs. We had been warned about a patch of quicksand that lay below that. A dog had at one time wandered into the mire, and had been sucked into the quicksand rapidly, and of course, died. I looked toward that area, and there was John, standing at the very edge of that patch. I opened my mouth and called "JOHN! JOHN!" My voice was a loud bellow. I scrambled down through the brush and nettles, repeating John's name in my miraculously loud voice, and he turned to look at me. Within seconds, I had him in my arms. I was covered with scratches and cuts. "What's wrong, Mama?" John asked, frightened. I was about to explain to him once more, a warning he had previously heard, but again I had no voice. Just a whisper.

If I had gone with my neighbor, I would have taken John and Kristin with me, and this frightening episode would not have happened. I took it as an omen that I should study Spanish.

The Wives

The initial briefing of wives consisted of a talk given by "the colonel" at the CIA headquarters in Langley. He informed us that we were privileged to be married to the "cream of the cream of the cream of the crop," having been selected from thousands of applicants.

We were advised that after our stay at the Farm, we had to discard any friendships we may have cultivated amongst ourselves, and furthermore, we must never acknowledge having met before, if by chance we ever saw each other in the future.

Strong bonds were inevitable. We were a small community

of women with no babysitters, no stores, no movies, and no restaurants. We relied on each other for company and conversation and shared childcare. When my mother died, one of my neighbors immediately offered to take care of our children, while I went to the funeral (with permission from the Man). She and I remained close friends for years. I always knew where she was stationed, and she always tried to keep track of me, and occasionally we would be in Washington at the same time. Behind closed doors we drank scotch and told our war stories. It was amazing how comical our lives seemed to us.

None of us had any idea what would be expected of us in our new environment of a foreign country. We were invited to a "seminar" given by a CIA woman, Miss B., who lived at the Farm. She was of a certain age, patrician and unmarried. She had been in the employ of the CIA since World War II, when it was called the OSS (Office of Strategic Services), and during which time she was reported to have parachuted into Belgium in the black of night. We did not know why, but we were a little uncertain about whether that qualified her to dispense advice on how to entertain at home in a foreign country. She advised us not to be anxious about the entertaining we would have to do, and that the best attitude was no attitude; that we "just be ourselves," without pretension. When one wife named Julie asked about our lack of good china and crystal, Miss B. assured us that cocktails could be served without apology, in whatever glasses we already had, to which Julie retorted: "In Captain Kangaroo cups?!"

Julie knew that in our new covert roles, we would always be, purportedly, families of successful businessmen, whose lifestyle was bordering on the sumptuous in a foreign country, with live-in maids and a social life that flourished. Our real income was low-grade government salary. A long way from a flourish.

There were no manuals or lectures explaining the decorum required when entertaining an army general in Madrid or a minister of education from Egypt or India. Where was the handbook to remind the hostess that certain religious teachings did not allow the consumption of shellfish, or meat, or alcohol? Or that chrysanthemums, while vividly attractive in the living room and dining room, were displayed only at funerals in Spain? Or that a gentleman kisses only the hand of a married woman, and never do his lips touch her skin? (Frank never did learn this, and was in a constant frenzy of hand kissing in all countries. The ladies didn't complain.) It would have been a decided advantage to have the knowledge imparted from a CIA wife who had Been There, rather than a female paratrooper.

Could anyone guess that a lady attending church in Spain must always have her arms covered? And must be ever alert never to touch the bare feet of her servant in India? On the other hand, an Indian bride must kiss the bare feet of her mother-in-law. Sadly for the bride, particularly if she was not Indian, there was never an overpowering urge to do this. Nor did I fight any urge that I had to touch the bare feet of my servant.

Paramilitary Training

This was an elective adjunct to intelligence training. At 11:00 p.m. we could hear the loud barking of dogs and the bullhorn shouts of the paramilitary instructors. Searchlights were arcing all over the compound. This seemed to be some kind of drill which would have been useful as a preview for guerrilla warfare, so I was perplexed. Why did Frank elect to take this course? He said it was an experience he just couldn't miss, even though he knew it would not be applicable in his own career. (More testosterone, of course.)

This exercise was not playing cops and robbers, but guerrillas and assassins. Few of the trainees were over thirty, so they had the energy and enthusiasm to enjoy being shot at while jumping over barbed wire fences (or plunging straight into them), trying to outrun the trained dogs that also pursued them. There was an absence of Old School Tie men here. Those men looked forward to being posted in a large city, wearing Brooks Brothers suits, carrying smooth-as-butter briefcases from their quaint European houses to their splendid offices downtown. Although this would be Frank's future as well, these exercises were too exciting for him to pass up. We never did hear anything about the other men who took the course because they were training for a different type of future, a rougher, wilder career path, useful in jungles that were not asphalt.

Later in the summer, the paramilitary trainees were told they would be taken on a three-week sortie in an unknown place: literally unknown. They were flown in a plane with black windows, fitted with parachutes, knives, and military gear, and dropped into a jungle. They were not allowed to carry any food, not even candy, or even a tea bag.

There were two paramilitary teams dropped in different locales, and they were to reach a destination without any supply of food or water. The other team was experienced. The teams were to destroy or be destroyed, and to eat and drink what they could find. As chance would have it, Frank's team found a lethargic snake, which was apparently not too well, so they caught and carried it in a large net for the evening meal. Frank was one of the carriers, and he tried to mask his revulsion. When the snake was barbecued for their first meal, Frank said he wasn't hungry. That evening, they were charged by a large wild boar, causing them to scatter snake kabobs as they fled—except for one lithe hero of American Indian heritage, who faced the boar and stabbed it enthusiastically enough to give everyone a head start.

The suggestion that they should kill the boar and cut it up for food was not viable when a vote was taken. Berries and leaves and ailing snakes would have to do. The heat, the dirt, the insects large and small, the constant fear of snakes, the skin rashes, the intestinal upheavals, all were a constant. One of the men collapsed early in the game, a victim of violent diarrhea as well as severe trauma, which so terrified him that he was returned to the station in a state of near hysteria, an understandable reaction, but of course, a personal disgrace never mentioned again. He nevertheless became a very good intelligence officer and a highly respected man with a gift for language.

When the black-windowed plane returned, wives were informed that they would be allowed to go to the landing point to meet their husbands. That in itself was a momentous occasion, as the landing strip was always off-limits and its cargo and passengers were top secret. This was to be a very busy day for me, as I was the self-appointed hairdresser and wanted to ensure we would all be suitably puffed and sprayed while we awaited the plane. The plane door opened, and one by one emerged emaciated, grey-bearded, and weary travellers. We honestly didn't recognize them. They were gaunt, but also triumphant. They had defeated the other team, no small feat in light of the fact that the other team was comprised of experienced guerrillas. The instructors were proud.

At a much later date, they were told they had been in Panama.

Dead Drops

This was the term used to describe the delivery or receipt of messages passed to or from an agent to the intelligence officer. For example, if Frank needed information about a particular topic, he would call his agent, use a code word that the agent already understood, and this meant that they were to exchange information at a particular magazine stand. There were different code words used for different locations.

This is how it worked: Frank would go to a newsstand, carrying the latest issue of *Time* magazine. Tucked inside Frank's *Time* magazine was a message for the agent. When the agent arrived at the magazine stand, he would peruse various magazines near *Time*. Frank would pick up a new *Time* magazine, and when no one was looking, put the one he was carrying at the top of the stack. The agent would pick up that magazine and take it to the cashier, and Frank, after browsing and perhaps buying another magazine as well as a *Time*, would pay the cashier and leave. When the agent had the information in writing, he would call Frank with his own code word: the little charade would be reversed. This was remarkably easy to do.

While at the Farm, a "dead drop" test was exercised in New York City. Future spies were exposed to this large city as a way to prepare them for the environs in which they would actually do dead drops in the future. (In whatever country, we were always located in the capital city.)

In the exercise in New York, instructors would play the part of agents. An instructor would call a public phone, the number of which had been noted, and Frank would be waiting to answer it and hear the code word. He would then go to the newsstand, park bench, subway station, or other location designated by the password. The instructor was actually following Frank. Now Frank had to perform the dead drop, constantly looking over his shoulder to see if he was being followed, stopping at store windows to check the reflection of anyone behind him, or ducking into a store on the way, for a matter of minutes, to elude his "shadow." Frank said this first exercise was remarkably unnerving. Four of the dead droppers were caught. Even a simple exercise like this could be blown. There were times in the years to come, when I carried out the dead drop, because Frank could not get away, or did not want to be seen. On these few occasions, I was nervous . . . but I could not deny that it was exciting.

In the ensuing years, a representative of the CIA would occasionally visit us and bring "toys" (as we called them) to demonstrate new and secret forms of communication. The man who did this was always personable, and was usually our guest for dinner. When he was there, it was almost like we were playing a children's game. He demonstrated a letter written in invisible ink, which when covered with a solution, would become visible. A thick ballpoint pen was actually a camera. Frank was given a new briefcase with a false bottom, which could be opened only by applying pressure at delicately placed locations. There was also a miniature camera, easily carried to take pictures of documents in a matter of seconds. There was also a thermos, commonly carried by people who brought their lunch to work, and this, too, had a false bottom, which could hold the tiny camera, as well as the film. It was cunningly made, and seemed weightless and noiseless.

There were no guns or weapons of any kind. In fact, if any of us had owned a gun, it would have been necessary to turn it in. My apologies to Sean Connery.

Leaving the Farm

When Frank graduated from the Farm, we were surprised to hear that there would actually be a graduation ceremony, such as it was. It apparently was a very guarded celebration of all the new intelligence officers and it was held in the mess hall of the compound. We were told that the colonel from Langley would be there to shake hands, after which many drinks would be consumed. This occasion was only for the men, and did not include their wives or families. Frank was not interested in attending, because the very confines described seemed to him to mark a hollow occasion, and then his instructor said, "You know, Frank, this will be the only time you will ever be recognized by anybody in this outfit, and the only time you will be praised by anybody here." Frank thought that was not a very compelling reason to sit in the mess hall and drink with the boys, because drinking with the boys had never been big on his schedule, unless the boys were fighter pilots in the Marine Corps. Plus, at age 29, he was the old man of the class, and he was exhausted. He said he just wanted to stay home and have a martini with his wife. It was a dear thing to do. Later in the evening there was a jolly banging on our door, which revealed two happily inebriated classmates, who had stopped to tell Frank that he had been one of the top ten in his class. Of course, he was pleased.

Our time at the Farm had not been difficult for me. Apart from missing Frank, the wives and families had become friendly, and had taken an interest in each other's problems. We had shared long evenings, and the children had found playmates. My next-door neighbor came over for coffee every morning, bringing her children along, and I looked forward to her company.

It is strange to realize that I never saw her again, and never heard any news of where they had been posted.

Frank had definitely made up his mind about working under deep cover, and his instructor said that someone was needed in Spain, but they had not yet found a cover company to make this possible. Nevertheless, he advised Frank to wait, and arrangements would be made for him to attend Berlitz language classes for as long as it took for them to find a host company. "You can live wherever you want," he said, "we'll store your furniture here." He said we would be paid a per diem for cost of living expenses, and that this amount would cover our rent.

Excellent. We could go back to San Francisco, and live in a motel with our two children, and say to our friends, "We're hoping Frank gets a job in Madrid, so he's going to study Spanish until he sees an ad in the paper for a job in Spain. No, we don't have any furniture, but this little motel is just swell." As ludicrous as this sounds, these are exactly the circumstances in which we found ourselves. During the next year, we moved into and out of five different furnished "places," as well as one beautiful house offered to us by a friend.

Frank was the eternal optimist, and even as the weeks and months passed, he simply "knew we would hear next week," and we would begin our exciting adventure. He just couldn't wait to start playing the game. It seemed to me that it would have been more realistic to keep us at the Farm, employing Frank as an instructor's assistant, for the sake of cover. I expect that this was a precedent they could not allow.

Limbo

During our wait to find a cover company, we moved in and

out of houses that would never appear in *Architectural Digest*. We stayed in the same area, but finding a furnished house for any period of time was almost impossible because our agenda was so mysterious that we could not lease a place for even six months. Frank bought a used car that allowed us mobility and transportation to and from his daily classes at Berlitz. Living in the same vicinity as our friends again was a mixed blessing. It was nearly impossible to explain our lifestyle and it was embarrassing.

During this long recess, we experienced one of our most difficult periods of trickery that would become our full-time occupation, just explaining what was happening in our lives, and why we were so displaced. And we found we were good at it. We made vague references to our fictitious employer, which we decided to call "Acme" and something, importers and exporters. We thought he could say he was involved in that line of work without revealing any details, and nobody would ask about the details. No one did. We also considered saying that Frank was going to be a "consultant," a title that to this day means nothing to me and more than likely, means nothing to the "consultant." "I'm kind of hurt that nobody has enough interest to quiz me," Frank said, "and I'm all prepared to give an answer."

During that pause in our life, I found that I was pregnant, which was a source of joy to us because we had planned to have three children. It did throw a wrench into some of our activities, as it was a difficult pregnancy because I was sure I was carrying a kick-boxer, deft at hitting the sciatic nerve. This brought me to my knees in a department store once, sending the other customers fleeing from the scene of an impromptu birth in the men's underwear section.

I had begun studying Spanish with a tutor, early every morning, which was not the best time for a nauseated mother-to-be.

The tutor was an American who had lived in Spain, and he treated us to the strong espresso Spaniards drink, sending my senses reeling with nausea.

One time, we lived in a spacious and beautiful house, lent to us by a friend who was going away for Christmas, thus allowing us to enjoy a terrific Christmas dinner with family and friends. It had a walk-in fireplace, with fieldstone rising to the ceiling, and a huge living room, which was perfect for an informal party on New Year's Eve. At that time, we had been in limbo for more than six months. My pregnancy allowed us a new story to tell: that we hoped we could stay in the United States for the birth, since conditions in Spain might be dicey. As a matter of fact, there was some truth to the story, as my obstetrician had suggested that childbearing in Spain would be about as up-to-date as spawning my child in an open field somewhere. (This turned out to be wrong from all points of view, which we discovered after living in Spain. We found that their obstetrical care was far superior to ours, involving the participation of the father, and keeping the newborn in a small bassinette beside the mother for several days.)

There was a telephone number that Frank would call on a regular basis, to see if there was any news about our future. We lived very frugally, and were unable to save or invest, which was a precursor that applied to the rest of our lives together. Frank was able to cushion the coffers by exercising his duty with the Marine Corps Reserve. He was flying out of a base on the east coast when he called me, jubilantly relaying the incredible news that we had a cover company to take us to Madrid, and that we were to prepare to move to their headquarters in the Midwest while he trained for his new cover job.

It was sweet relief when we moved into a charming little house. The house had at one time been the chauffeur's lodging on an old estate. It had a slanted roof that gave the upstairs bedrooms charm, and we were again surrounded with our own furniture. I grew to love that house, and nested so intensely that I actually baked bread. I remember looking out the window at the changing leaves, and smelling the bread baking while John and Kristin were napping. I was content.

My late pregnancy was difficult, as I experienced false labor every few days, finding myself doubling over in the kitchen and watching the hands of the clock, then finding it was a false alarm. When the actual day of birth arrived, Johanna came into the world without the attendance of the doctor, but we did make it to the hospital.

We desperately needed to establish some kind of permanence in our lives. Over one year had passed since we'd left the Farm and we had been homeless for two Christmases.

The insanity was just beginning and we were gathering no moss.

The Briefing

While waiting for the necessary paperwork to be activated, as well as the medical examinations, we lived in a small furnished apartment outside of Washington. Frank had a lot of meetings with unnamed people who explored the intricacies of his job, and his role to play, and then they asked to have an interview with me. I was very fatigued, and at the same time quite nervous about this briefing. I looked at it as a possible interrogation. If I struck them as unsatisfactory material, another wife would be supplied.

Johanna was still being fed three or four times a night. This was long before daddies did any daddying; all ministering to the child was for the person who gave birth. I was exhausted. Upon seeing my reflection in the mirror, I decided that wearing a hat would be a fine addition toward appearing to be a lady of not only style, but class. Good enough to be married to this man. On my last frenzied whirl around the apartment, I discovered that Kristin and John had put apples and oranges in the toilet. My first reaction was to start screaming, so I took a Valium. A blue one. Then I ran for the bus.

It was a cold and blustery February day, and the run for the bus cleared my head. The office to which I was going had a fictitious name. When I entered the building, I found it on the vestibule directory, and when I approached the door, I wondered if I should just walk in or knock. I knocked. The door opened and I was greeted by three gentlemen who offered me a chair at a conference table. I removed my coat, but kept the hat on for effect.

One of the men started to tell me about the history of Spain, going several kings back in time. The radiators hissed. It was very hot and this man was very boring. Between the hissing and the interminable history lesson, I realized that I was nodding off. My hat had a very large brim, and I actually felt it barely touch the table as I nodded. The Valium was a mistake.

I was being asked a question. What? For the sake of my own pride, and not for them, I asked if they could tell me anything about conditions in Spain in *this* century, such as housing, medical care, schools. This was a mistake. One of the other men began his little lecture, and took to his feet, walking back and forth with his hands behind his back, droning about I know-not-what. I tried very hard to stay awake. I expected Peter Sellers to enter and finish the scene.

I learned nothing. I expect they might have thought I was drunk, regardless that it was nine o'clock in the morning. For God's sake, I thought, why wouldn't they find a woman who had lived in Spain to tell me about the fundamentals? Hearing about King Felipe in another century would not get me through a day in Madrid (and they didn't even tell me the interesting part, that he died of syphilis).

Two hours later, I stumbled down to the street and caught a cab.

Well, at least I had a morning without children, I said to myself. That was a weird trio of whoever they were. I wondered if any one of them had ever been to Spain.

Leaving the U.S.

Before we left for Spain, we were instructed to go to Washington so that each of us could undergo a medical examination. This was the custom for all CIA personnel before being stationed in a foreign country. Our accommodations during the stay consisted of one room with two double beds at Howard Johnson. This was for five people, including a three-month-old. Despite Frank's plea for two adjoining rooms, we were told that this could not be authorized because three small children should be able to fit in one double bed. It was necessary for us to request a small crib for Johanna.

In order to turn on the television or go to the bathroom, we had to walk across the beds. At this point, I fell apart. Johanna was still waking four times a night and sleep for anyone was impossible. Not only did the beds take up all the floor space, there was no place for us to put twelve suitcases. Our suitcases were large, as we'd been told our furniture would not arrive in Madrid for some time. We had to pile the suitcases on the beds. This certainly did not augur well for what we might expect in the future. There was no consideration for the eighteen months we had just spent literally homeless. Pregnancy and a new baby and two toddlers are difficult enough in one's own home with all its creature comforts, but under the circumstances we had had to accept, it had been misery. I felt we could have appealed more strongly to someone for my sake and for the children, but Frank was not a boat-rocker, particularly at this embryonic stage of his career. It seemed clear to me that there was no personal interest taken in the case of people like us. It was By The Book.

We were told to be at the doctor's office, en masse, at 11:00 a.m. on a Thursday. We were further told that our appointment would be under the name of McKenzie, so that no records would be on file under our real names. Of course, our toddlers, who were not crazy about doctors, asked why we had to go if nobody was sick, and we gave them a vague explanation. The office was in a basement apartment in a residential area. We sat in a small waiting area and caught a glimpse of the doctor as a patient left his examining room. He was white-haired, stooped, and wearing a white coat. I figured he was probably a retired doctor who did only this kind of examination. When the receptionist called the name of McKenzie we rose to our feet and John, our three-year-old, said loudly, "That's not for us! That's not our name!" I held his wrist very tightly and steered him into the doctor's examining room.

Our physical examinations were so cursory as to be a joke. Look down the throat, say "aaah." Look in the ears. Hit the knee with the mallet. Listen to the breathing. One of us could have had leukemia or bleeding ulcers or a brain tumor, and we would have been pronounced as fine specimens and allowed to leave the country. Every two years hence we were subjected to these comical physicals when we had home leave, and we were never able to persuade the powers in Washington that it would be far more feasible to see a doctor in the area in which we lived. Ah, but if we did, my migraines and menstrual cramps might have become public knowledge.

When we had cleared the health hazard, we prepared to leave. I didn't know how to handle three children on such a long flight, so I planned ahead, forever organized. I had bought an innovative "leash" for both John and Kristin. I thought it would solve the problem of either one of them wandering off. The leashes were made of small straps, which fit around the child's wrist and then hooked to spiral cords that resembled telephone cords. Each leash was then attached to another band around my own wrist. I thought this would keep my little people near me while I held Johanna, who was four months old.

We knew nothing about customs and passport control, and Frank looked after these formalities while I waited. John and Kristin loved their leashes, and almost immediately stretched them as far as they would go, then ran around me in circles. This should have been comic relief, as the coils were all tangled together. I had no sense of humor at that particular point, and I lapsed into tears. The Three Stooges.

What the hell was I doing, standing in an airport with three small children and a crazy husband who was taking us to a foreign place where we didn't know the language? It was like being caught in the middle of a bad dream, never to wake up. We should have been in a sunny town in California, deciding which preschool would suit the children and not hanging on to them with leashes.

Spain (1964-1972)

Arriving in Spain

Being a good mother was of paramount importance to me. I loved my children fiercely, and whatever upheaval we experienced, my first consideration was the children: that they would have space, and always feel safe. Johanna was a happy baby, easy to look after. Our first dreaded plane trip to Madrid was not the nightmare I thought it could be. We sat behind the bulkhead, and the stewardess brought a basket for Johanna to sleep in, which sat at my feet. The changing of cloth diapers was a messy and odiferous business, and I tried to avoid looking at the passengers nearby. John and Kristin sat together with coloring books and actually liked the flight. I looked forward to the suite in our hotel, which had been reserved by the Agency.

When we arrived in Madrid, and registered in the truly quaint apartment/hotel complex, it was more thrilling than I had expected it to be. It was a beautiful city, and from customs through cab drivers and hotel personnel, the Spaniards appeared to be a courteous and congenial people. When our luggage arrived and I began the ritual of counting the suitcases, I realized to my horror that my brilliant idea of packing all the diapers in one large bag had backfired. It was the only bag that had gone to Switzerland. (At that time, there was no such thing as a disposable diaper.) The housekeeper at the hotel spoke English, and she was an enormous help, supplying me with towels until the next day when the airlines returned the lost bag.

We had an old-fashioned suite of rooms with a balcony that overlooked one of the most beautiful streets in Madrid. My major discovery when I appraised the hotel facilities was that there was no laundry room, and Madrid had no laundromats. I tried not to acknowledge the washboard that was part of the huge kitchen sink, but I had to face reality, and diapers needed to be washed. Our hotel allowance did not cover laundry. Once more our living room and dining room were festooned with drying diapers, draped on chairs and hanging from tables.

We had also been told that the reason we had a suite was because we were not allowed restaurant privileges and could therefore make use of the kitchen. The largest utility in the kitchen was an enormous wood stove. This, I thought, was taking "quaint" too far. A business executive would not have been deprived in this way. In the days that followed, we discovered that this was a family hotel. We met other people of every nationality, all with children, and I was the only woman who did not send diapers to the hotel laundry.

I learned how to shop for groceries, bobbing along with a borrowed pram provided by the housekeeper, with a new infant and two toddlers, going from tiny shop to tiny shop. This was a clumsy business when I discovered that shopkeepers in Madrid did not have paper bags. Eggs were wrapped in newspaper, and the long, fragrant loaves of bread were deposited in the pram. I tried to treat this as an adventure, as the children were greeted with cheerful clucking and pinching of cheeks, extolling the angelic blond beauty at every shop on the street.

I needed help. I needed advice.

Waiting

We had expected someone from the U.S. Embassy to contact us at our hotel, in order to brief Frank about assignments and "targets," but we did not hear from anyone. Frank was prohibited from approaching the embassy, but had been told that his case officer was going to be a new man in Madrid. There were no messages. We floated in limbo and wondered how we would pay the hotel bill, since he had received no salary. (We heard later that we had been "lost in the files." It appeared that nobody knew we were there.)

I learned how to say, "Is this house for rent?" in Spanish, and began house hunting. Because I had to take the children with me, I was restricted to the vicinity of the hotel, which was such a beautiful area that it would have been my number one choice anyway. Whenever I saw workmen by a house that looked empty, I asked my memorized question, but was not prepared for the onslaught of rapid Spanish replies or explanations. I soon realized that the Spanish people are verbose and cheerful and loved children. Their ebullience won me over, but I still had no idea what houses were for rent.

While we waited for contact from the embassy, Frank began to feel apprehensive about his future relationship with his case officer. He knew it would make his job much easier if they had a kinship, and Frank hoped he wouldn't be the stiff kind of government type we had at times encountered. When Frank finally received a phone call from his case officer, he was asked to be at a certain street corner at a certain time. He would recognize his contact by his furled umbrella and red tie. Frank recognized him immediately. As they began to cross the street together, a Mercedes almost plowed through the intersection. "What do you think you're doing, you fucking Nazi?!" the case officer yelled, hitting the windshield with the umbrella. "This is a crosswalk!" At that moment, Frank knew he liked this man a lot. Indeed, it was the beginning of a long-term friendship between them, not to mention between our families.

During our stay at the hotel, the children played on the large balcony overlooking the street, a favorite place for John to "fly" his little balsam airplane, which was held together with rubber bands. I worried that he might lose it on the street. One day, he came to me and very seriously told me that his plane had flown up to the next floor, and that the man who lived there had stolen it. I had no idea what that was all about, and I was concerned that John had perhaps annoyed the man above us, so I went up the stairs with him, and knocked on the door of the unit above ours. The man who opened the door was Henry Fonda.

"My son lost a small airplane that he was playing with. I'm sorry to bother you, but he thinks you might have seen it," I said. Mr. Fonda replied that he hadn't seen it, and I apologized for bothering him. When I took John's hand to go downstairs, Mr. Fonda was still standing in the doorway, and John said loudly, "He's a liar."

Gypsy Children

During our nomadic year and a half, John and Kristin were wonderful. All the moves could have resulted in a complete loss of any sense of security, but there was no evidence of that. Giving birth to two children in one year was very taxing for me. I worshipped sleep. I was staggering with exhaustion most of the time, and some of the time I was a cranky mother, but I knew it was necessary to be strict about their behavior and to display my love at the same time, constantly telling them how good they were. For the most part, I had to be both mother and father to them during Frank's frequent absences, but when he was home, he was a gentle and caring father.

The up side to having two children in a row is that they became pals. Bringing home a newborn does not cause trauma to a one-year-old. From the time Kristin could walk, she was dogging John's footsteps, and he didn't mind. That was a blessing for me, in spite of small incidents when they were found methodically painting the wall with honey and peanut butter. They loved each other then, and they have a special bond to this day, having faced the hostile world of new schools and new countries together. They accepted their baby sister with very little interest and no jealousy.

The Cover Office

Frank found himself in a touchy situation in the Madrid cover office. He was to replace an elderly Spanish manager, who had been employed in that capacity for many years, and when Frank arrived, he discovered that this gentleman, Sr. Sanchez, had not been notified that Frank was going to join the office, far less that he was going to be replaced—by an American. Pride is everything to a Spaniard. Frank was very uncomfortable about his job with an entirely Spanish staff, none of whom spoke English, but the delicacy required in dealing with Sr. Sanchez was extremely dicey.

The president of the American company was a very wealthy man who could be described as a playboy, and between his golf and skiing commitments, he paid little attention to business. He had simply neglected to advise Sr. Sanchez. Given the cultural awkwardness, Frank felt he really should have made a trip to Madrid to explain to Sr. Sanchez that he indeed was being replaced. Frank's insinuating himself into the office staff made Sr. Sanchez angry and he made no effort to cover up his hostility, treating Frank like a clerk, to be easily dismissed.

When the situation was finally clarified by a phone call, Sr. Sanchez was enraged and insulted. How could he be dismissed at all, far less be replaced by an American upstart? This was particularly hard for Frank because he could understand, and there was no way to ingratiate himself. Sr. Sanchez's revenge was to obscure the order and contents of files, as well as to completely destroy the telephone index, leaving Frank totally in the dark about his job.

Fortunately, Frank's grace won over the office staff. They sympathized with his situation and after a short while, he discovered that they all hated Sr. Sanchez, who had been a brusque and cavalier taskmaster. Frank instigated regular staff luncheons at a good restaurant, with everyone in the office attending, and in that way they began to feel at ease with him. They did everything they could to help him.

Home

I found a house. It was three stories high with small bedrooms and a den. It charmed me. It was so Spanish, with its tiled floors and interior walls, all with simple white plaster. It was in a Spanish neighborhood lined with big leafy trees. There was a high wall around the garden, and just outside the back door there was a fig tree, an apricot tree, rosebushes, and a perfect place to put swings. All the rooms were small, as they are in authentic Spanish houses, but there was enough room off the kitchen for an American washer and dryer! Hallelujah! Apart from this, we would have the entire Spanish experience.

There were some comforts that we missed, but they were

insignificant. There was only one bathroom, for example, with a bidet. (An American friend who lived in an apartment had turned her bidet into a planter, thereby missing one of the finer things of life.) Without self-consciousness, the children picked up whole chunks of Spanish phrases while playing *futbol* (soccer) on the street with the neighbors' children. What a wonder to have found a house where children played in the street, going in and out of each other's houses, always being chided by the maid in a strident voice, who very graphically addressed one small boy as *mucosa* (mucousy) because his nose was always running, and another as *gordo*, which means fat. Their little psyches did not seem to be at all damaged by this lack of respect. Spaniards' use of language is not known for nuances.

We were glad to move into a neighborhood of old and charming houses, although most of our American friends lived in another area near the American school or in apartments with a lot of other English-speaking people. At times, I envied the convenience they enjoyed, but when they visited us, they always exclaimed how much they liked our house.

We spent five months in the hotel, waiting for our furniture to arrive, and during that period of time we made friends with families of every nationality who also stayed in the hotel. We hosted a cocktail party and invited everyone in the hotel, which was an excellent mesh of people, and who became our good friends over a number of years, giving us an entrée into a number of different cultures and a varied group of people. I was happy. We had a home. And we had friends.

Just around the corner from our house was a school run by Dominican nuns, which was a combination nursery school and elementary school. John's friends in the neighborhood attended this school, and in September, they were preparing for the school year, and being measured for their uniforms. It occurred to us that our children had spent every day since we arrived with these friends, chattering in Spanish, no matter how mangled. The kids didn't care. What if we sent them to that school? Could it hurt them? How difficult might it be? I approached the good nuns about the possibility of our foreign towheads going to their school. They clapped their hands with enthusiasm and almost insisted that they come. They beamed and gestured with outstretched arms that our *rubios* (blonds) would be more than welcome.

On the day school started, I left John and Kristin holding hands in line, looking stoic and pale, like frightened waifs, surrounded by those blackhaired children, noisily communicating in rapid Spanish. What had I done? I ran home and burst into tears. I called Frank, weeping. I watched the clock. I had to control myself from rushing back to the school and pulling my children out of the schoolyard, back to the safety of our walled garden. It was years before John told me that on that first day, he didn't know how to ask about the bathroom. He wet his pants and had been punished! I felt like killing myself when I found that out. I was such a terrible woman.

We soon found out that preschool in Spain was not finger painting or watching puppets. It was reading, writing, and arithmetic. A Spanish child cannot enter first grade until he can read and write. It was the opening of an entire new vista, particularly for Kristin, who loved books and now could read them by herself. She became a voracious reader, and ultimately read all the Enid Blyton books in Spanish. While I studied Spanish with a tutor, I was both intimidated and proud when the children corrected my grammar and pronunciation. (To this day, John, a grown man, says he does math in his head in Spanish.)

Good To Be Me

Being the boss's wife was a new experience for me. As far as the Spanish staff was concerned, I played no role at all. They were cordial and courteous when I came to the office, which was infrequently. When the company president visited Spain, he came for frolic and fun; his wife came for the shopping. I, the lowly manager's wife, was summoned to do her bidding. That is, to accompany her to boutiques, translate for her, and dash around the shop while she was in the fitting room shouting orders to me. She was rude and loud if she ever had to interface with the very chic clerks, but none of this bothered me, because I was really somebody else; I wasn't the woman she assumed me to be. I didn't give a damn whether she liked or approved of me. Ass kissing wasn't on my schedule, nor was it on Frank's, although he did go out of his way willingly when they were in town, and he genuinely enjoyed spending time with his playboy boss.

On one shopping outing, Mrs. President glanced at her watch and dismissed me when it was time for lunch, informing me she might need me later in the day. I put her in a cab and told the driver her destination, a very expensive restaurant. She joined her husband and his friends there, including Frank, who had arranged the lunch. He was stunned when she arrived without me. When Mr. President asked her where I was, she shrugged and said she didn't know. If this had been a "real" situation, I would have been humiliated, but I did have the best of both worlds, so her attitude didn't matter to me. She was in no way an influence in our lives, and no pandering was required, although it was definitely expected.

Frank was angry about my not being invited to lunch; it was something he had taken for granted. In this particular instance, I had the luxury of vehemently disliking the boss's wife, and not letting it affect me. It was my first brush with the corporate world, and I could see the advantage of ours, by comparison. I was at home when Mrs. President called later in the afternoon. I told the maid to say I was out. Rah.

I was keenly aware of the drudgery required of embassy wives, who were forced to entertain "properly," and more than just occasionally. I was immune to that suffering as well. I was under deep cover and I was glad.

I remember when an American family moved in across the street. They had a son John's age. John asked him, "Do you know how to speak Spanish?" and the boy replied, "No. How?" The boy's father was a colonel in the Air Force and because there was no vacancy at the Air Force base, they had been forced to take a house in the city. His wife was so terrified at having been separated from the American base that she never left the house alone in the entire year that they lived there. There were numerous shops within walking distance, but she would venture no farther than my house gate.

She had lived in another foreign country, but only in military housing There, every one was American and everything she needed was nearby, including a movie theater, restaurant and bar, and swimming pool. When she needed any bread or bakery goods, she asked me to buy it for her. Otherwise, every Saturday she went with her husband to the base to shop at the commissary. She always generously asked if there was anything she could buy for me there, but I had no trouble finding everything we needed in the local markets. If her doorbell rang, she phoned me to come over to see what they wanted, because she didn't understand the language. She never imagined what she was missing, and she returned to the United States without having brushed with the lifestyle of Spain and its people. Her memory of Madrid would be of the delicious bread from the corner market, a store she had never seen.

The Contessa

Our Spanish tutor had been recommended to Frank by one of the people in his office who was acquainted with her. Her name was Carmen and she professed to be a countess. She introduced us to a varied group of people in the Spanish community, which was, at times, agony for me, as I wondered if I would ever speak Spanish well enough to get through a dinner party without a migraine headache. Hosting a dinner in our home, it was both interesting and insulting to note how the Countess would very openly snap her fingernail against the rim of the wine glass to test the "ping" that identifies good crystal, or how, when seated at the dinner table, she would turn over the plate to see how our china rated. We had come beyond Captain Kangaroo glasses, but not much. We were a long way from English china and Swedish crystal.

I was surprised at how easily impressed Frank was by the "Contessa." Her arrogance annoyed me, and her attitude, as she swept by or ignored people, was embarrassing to me. This kind of attitude is called *muy flamenco* in Spain. It is a visual description of the dramatic disdain and pomposity of the flamenco dancer. She had insinuated herself into our lives without invitation, and certainly without any sign of graciousness on my part, but she was oblivious to that. I was disappointed that Frank didn't see through her.

One day, Frank came home beaming, because Carmen, the Contessa, had invited us all to go to Leon for the weekend to meet her children. I was not prepared to spend four days with people who didn't speak any English, when I myself could not speak Spanish, except for a few simple phrases. I did not want to face four days in a hotel room with children under any circumstances, and certainly not with an infant. Despite my protests, Frank insisted that we take this opportunity, because she was an invaluable contact. After a year at Berlitz and daily tutoring, Frank could get along well in Spanish and was looking forward to meeting more rich people. I should have said, "Take the children and go. I'll stay home." The contacts for Frank's career had taken top billing in his life.

On the morning that we stocked the station wagon, picked up Carmen, and started the long drive, I was very unhappy. Her nonstop talking, punctuated with slapping my shoulder from the back seat, was building a rage inside me. I looked out the window and let the tears slide down my face. If Frank noticed, he didn't show it. I again realized that I was not number one on his priority list. I think I was angrier with Frank by then than I was with Carmen.

Carmen's family members were nice, hospitable people, apparently of some social status, judging from their beautifully appointed home and many servants. They "raised horses," which I have always considered to be high tone. I found it easier to make an attempt at communication after I had a couple of drinks, because I lost my reservation, and whenever words failed me, I tried to act out the message I was trying to convey. They were highly amused. That was when I discovered that liquor could blur the edges of my fears and apprehension. I thought I was amusing, and I was no longer angry with Frank.

El Gato

Our first all-Spanish evening at our home was memorable. We were entertaining members of Carmen's family, to reciprocate their great generosity in Leon. I was tense with anxiety, still unsure of myself with the language. It was a chilly November evening, and we had a roaring fire in the fireplace. I had already placed hors d'oeuvres on the coffee table, canapés I had agonized over and prepared myself. Small pots of caviar and sour cream, chopped onion and hard-boiled egg, smoked salmon with triangles toast. The candles were lit. The silver was gleaming. The maid had shrieked upon seeing the chrysanthemums, and their funereal presence had been quickly removed.

The doorbell rang, fashionably late, and Frank and I both stood at the door to greet our guests. The first one was Manolo, Carmen's son. He was carrying a bouquet of long-stemmed roses and an elaborate box of candy. He had swept in and was bowing to kiss my hand when a sudden screech came from the cat, which had been on the roof and had suddenly fallen down the chimney into the fire. The cat tore across the living room and hurtled into the dining room before Frank could douse her with water. Caviar flew into the air and onto the living room curtains, ashtrays were upside down on the carpet, the maid burst into tears, and Manolo was flat on his back in the dining room, having been knocked over by the blazing cat.

Still on his back, clutching his candy and convulsing with laughter, he chortled: "Que manera de romper el hielo!" (What a way to break the ice!) Indeed. It was the beginning of a fun-filled relationship with Manolo, and every time he visited us, he would dramatically peek around the front door and ask, "Donde esta el gato?" (Where is the cat?)

Fashionably Late

Dinner in Madrid was served at around 10:00 p.m. with cock-tails at 9:00. These hours made sense to Spaniards because all business was closed between two in the afternoon until five, remaining open until eight, and the doors of the office did not open until ten in the morning. These hours suited Frank and me well, because we were both night people, but it was terribly hard for most expatriates, especially if they were early-to-bed people. The Spaniards also enjoyed *merienda* (something like high tea) at five in the afternoon, thereby carrying them through until the late dinner hour. Even children were on this time schedule. The common snack for children was a large slice of French bread with a solid piece of chocolate in the middle, which without doubt kept them on a sugar high until the next meal. I had to make sure that the maid didn't offer this to our children.

At times, when we were with American friends having dinner in a restaurant, it was obvious that they were fighting sleep when there was still another course to be served. It would have been difficult enough to wait such a long time for dinner without consuming alcohol, but cocktails were served and many wines were consumed, adding, of course, to the sleepiness. Once, when we had American houseguests, they asked if we would mind going to a restaurant at an earlier time, and were stunned to hear that no restaurant began to serve dinner until after nine.

The hours between two and five were still called "siesta" time, but this nap was not routine with the people we knew. On the day we moved into the house, I was bustling along with the movers, giving directions as best that I could, and then suddenly realized they had all disappeared. I looked around and saw them nowhere, despite their truck still parked on the street. I walked out to the street, and there they all were, lying on the grass by the sidewalk, sleeping. I was shocked . . . who did they think they were? I methodically marched down the sidewalk, kicking at their feet and saying "Vamonos!," one term that I did know, meaning "Let's go!" They tipped back the peaks of their caps to see what insane person was bothering them and then calmly went back to sleep.

Mr. and Mrs. Spook

It was part of Frank's job to find and cultivate people who were in a position to acquire intelligence information that would be of help to the United States. He was not interested in acting upon anything that would be of harm to our host country. Throughout his career, Frank was instructed to gather information about dealings with Russia and Russia's alliances, whether commercial or military.

This was during the Cold War, when our country did not have friendly dealings with Russia, and with nuclear power in Russia's hands, we wanted to know whatever we could find out. Sources of information were manifold. Introductions to possible sources were intricate operations. Sometimes pure luck would intervene, and Frank would find himself in a position to court the friendship of someone who had access to information he needed. It frequently happened that these people became our friends. Not just Frank's, but ours. We were the instigators, but in time, friendship would deepen to such an extent that our family and their family would be inter-involved. They knew our children and we knew theirs. They came to John's first Holy Communion and we attended their son's wedding. We exchanged birthday and Christmas presents.

It would seem that because we truly liked these people, the job would be made easier. But how could we overlook the initial reason we spent time with them? How could we even think of the possibility of revelation that they were being used?

The friendship was real, as was our affection toward each other. Although what Frank was doing was in its own way noble, how could we justify our initial intention?

Because Frank was the manager of the Spanish branch of the American company he represented, he was able to hire anyone he chose, so valuable sources were put on the payroll, and actually did their jobs well, even traveling with Frank. In this way, they were paid for the information Frank gleaned from them. We had to dismiss any feelings of guilt by reminding ourselves that the end justified the means, and that the extrication of information hurt no one. We would converse and a tape recorder installed by a CIA "second story" man picked up the entire conversation. This could be done in a way that obliterated the music that was playing during the conversation.

Later, I would translate the tape and type the manuscript, a long and tedious job. I experienced a number of emotions while doing this, hearing the laughter, picking up the intimacy in the voice of the speaker, our friend, and the feeling of camaraderie that came through, and the trust. This is tacky, I thought. This is shameful. Difficult to justify. But it's only a job, only a job, only a job.

To oil the wheels, and to loosen the tongue, there was always a lot of alcohol consumed. First cocktails, then wine, then cognac with coffee. It wasn't until many years of experiencing this kind of emotional turmoil, toward the end of Frank's career, that I completely understood the need for the unusual clause in our health insurance with the CIA, which offered treatment for alcoholism or substance abuse, and psychiatric care. Frank and I became accustomed to drinking every day and the evening cocktail hour was a must, to calm the nerves. That cocktail "hour" often stretched to two. Over the years, I drank to excess and became clinically depressed. There are more alcoholics and more divorces in the CIA than in any other profession for which percentages are researched.

After Frank's retirement, when we found ourselves expected to live a normal life, the old habits died hard. Our lifestyle had been nefarious. When we made new friends, Frank would ask them dozens of questions, and was always a very good listener. That was not necessarily a bad thing, because people are flattered when given such attention. I felt he was just slipping into form, smooth as silk.

Several years after living in Spain, we heard that a Spanish friend whose voice we had recorded that evening had died of a heart attack. Frank received this news with calm and seemed unaffected, as though we had just listened to the weather report. That part of his life was over. He had compartmentalized his heart. This was the way he had reinvented himself.

The fabric of our connections with people who were useful to Frank was not easy for me to live with, because I was so close to it all the time. For the first time in my life I had begun to have severe tension headaches, so painful that I sought the advice of a neurologist. He injected novocaine, then cortisone into the knots of muscle. Of course, the headaches were stress induced. I had always been a healthy specimen in "our other life," as I called it. I also suffered frequent abdominal pain, particularly following a meal shared with Spanish friends, playing my deceptive role.

Having been known as a person so forthright to the point of abrupt, I was not suited to deception. There was just so much that could be pushed into the sub-conscious in the name of what we were supposed to consider as justice. This role would have been easier for a courtesan, vamping and mysterious. Frank was a spontaneous entertainer and I was a planner. I knew that he wished I were more unconstrained and impulsive, because he admired those characteristics in others. I was stuck with who I was. Sometimes I had the uneasy feeling that Frank would be happier with someone else. A role-player. Like him.

The Boris Episode

There were times when Frank needed my help, usually to translate intelligence memos written in Spanish. They could not be translated at the embassy, because there appeared to be no secretaries in the political section who could read and write Spanish. I was unable to help Frank in this way until I had been in Spain for a few years and felt confident about my ability to speak and socialize entirely in Spanish.

Once, there was an intriguing assignment for me. Frank had been meeting with a Spanish-speaking Russian, Boris, who was being highly paid by the CIA for his information. Frank was suspicious that Boris was a double agent, working both sides, as it were, so he asked for my help one evening. The plan was as follows: Boris would have coffee in a small café, taking a seat by the window where Frank could see him. Frank would then drive by the café in a particular Volkswagen. When Boris spotted the car going by, he would walk to a designated corner several blocks away and Frank would pick him up there.

When Boris exited the café, I was to walk a discreet distance behind, keeping a keen eye on him. I was to wear a black wig (which I borrowed from a friend "for a costume party") and an ankle-length brown coat. I would also carry a large black umbrella, which I would use like a walking stick. If Boris talked to anyone on the street, or made a phone call, I was to open the umbrella to signal Frank. This was a really sappy piece of drama, in my opinion.

Frank was carrying a German passport and wore a fake

mustache and thick glasses, as he did every time he met with Boris. When we drove away from our house in the Volkswagen, he said he wasn't feeling well. I suggested it was just nerves, or perhaps the thick glasses. A few minutes later, Frank shot his head out the window and vomited violently. This was not a good beginning, I thought. Definitely not good.

The café where we were to see Boris was on an intimate little street in a residential area. We parked nearby. Frank got out of the car with me and we sat on a bench so he could catch his breath. He threw up again. "Put your head down!" I ordered heartlessly, as though I were annoyed with him. I also ducked my head, thinking one of us might be recognized. I realized I was looking at the puddle of Frank's upheaval and his mustache was in it. I quickly picked up the mustache and slapped it on Frank's ashen upper lip, but it wouldn't stick. Half of it did, but the other half didn't. It hung down to his chin.

Boris wasn't by the café window yet. I could see a *farmacia* (drug store) sign across the way, so I bolted across the street, my long brown coat billowing behind me. Mission: adhesive tape. I quickly bought the tape and ran back. Folding the tape over, I was able to jam Frank's mustache back in place. He was so sick by now that he was trembling. He glanced up and raised his eyebrows. There was Boris in the café. Frank stood, staggered over to the Volkswagen, and pulled away.

I waited until Boris left the café, and then followed at a distance. It was a clear evening, filled with stars; the big black umbrella was a ludicrous accessory and would look even crazier if I opened it. Boris lit a cigarette and strolled down the street. He spoke to no one. I was not destined to be Mary Poppins tonight. After he got in the Volkswagen with Frank, I hailed a taxi to go home, removing my wig and coat to avoid suspicion when I arrived. The driver seemed to find this only mildly interesting. (We had donned our gay apparel in the garage before we left.)

Frank's plan after picking up Boris was to go to a hotel room in a very large and busy hotel. They would have their discussion there, as they had done on previous occasions. Earlier in the day, after booking the room with his German passport, Frank had rigged a reel-to-reel tape recorder behind the bed. (There was nothing simpler at that time.) He later told me that when they got to the hotel room, he was imploding with diarrhea and had to apologize to Boris for his nonstop trips to the bathroom. As he sat on the toilet, he imagined the whir-r-r-r of the tape and the impending doom if it reached an end and began to flap.

There was no way of turning the tape machine off without moving the bed, and he was becoming concerned. There was only one thing to do. He had to tell Boris how ill he was and arrange to meet him another time. Luckily, Boris had a written report to give him and didn't mind rescheduling their discussion. As soon as the door closed behind him, the tape started to flap.

Frank spent the following week in bed with stomach flu and high fever. Shaken, but not stirred.

Spooks at Work

Occasionally, we would enjoy a visit from a representative of the Washington office who was something like a roving ambassador for all the deep cover people like us who sometimes felt they were flotsam, forgotten, without any contact with the real world from which we were so separated. This man touched a number of bases throughout Europe and North Africa, dispensing goodwill and even praise. He was a wandering morale booster. We loved him. His name was Mark.

Whenever Mark visited us, he'd have dinner with us and

spend the evening. We had to be sure that friends didn't turn up and that the maid was out. Although he could easily have been introduced as our cousin Sam, we had to follow the "rules."

Mark had just been in Africa. He had never met the CIA deep cover case officer there, so he made meeting arrangements by creating precise steps for him to follow. They would meet casually and privately at the beach in the early evening. The man would be walking his large dog and would stop Mark to ask for a match to light his cigarette. Then they would talk.

Mark drove to the designated place in a rental car and brought sandwiches and drinks so they could safely conduct the meeting there without being seen. However, they had not taken into consideration the tide. When Mark looked toward the beach, he saw a man walking up to his shins in water, carrying an enormous dog over his shoulder. No one else was on the beach. Following instructions, they sloshed toward each other and when they met, the man asked Mark for a light. They then waded back up to the car. Mark had left the car windows open because it was so hot. When they approached, they saw that it was filled with baboons that had not only demolished the food with great glee, but had defecated everywhere to show their appreciation, their compliments to the chef. Baboons, he added when telling us this story, are irritable creatures, not easy to approach. These realities were a long way from the espionage fantasy of doing the tango in white tie and tails.

Boris, the Russian spy, remained with Frank for the remaining years we were in Spain. He was paid in American cash, and I was not aware if he was paid by the piece or by the hour, but I did know that Frank paid him in cash. One evening, Frank was carrying $5,000 in cash, which was folded into the daily Spanish newspaper. He had told Boris to be on a certain corner on a wide boulevard, and to watch for Frank, who would appear at the opposite corner. At a precise time, Frank would cross to the center of the island of the boulevard and place the newspaper in the litter can, with its headline clearly showing. Frank had been having a drink in a bar with his new case officer, Scott, a genial man with whom he got along very well. Frank glanced at his watch and invited Scott to walk around the block with him so he could do his "dead drop." He saw Boris at the other corner, and at the precise time, walked to the litter can and dropped the newspaper so the title could clearly be seen. Just as Frank was walking away from the can and Boris was walking toward the island, an empty city bus, its sign saying "Off Duty," suddenly came to a stop, and its driver jumped out and dashed toward the litter can, as he had noticed the late edition of the paper there. He snatched it up and jumped back on the bus. Frank and Scott watched in dumb shock, as did Boris (Russians were not known for their sense of humor).

Scott sat down on the curb with his head in his hands, shaking with laughter. Frank was speechless. He continued to stare, open-mouthed, at the place where the bus had been. "You're going to have to take a lot of taxis to cover this one," Scott gasped, referring cruelly to the long-standing complaint about the meanness of expense account allowances, and that taxi fares were the only item recognized.

When Frank came home, he could hardly tell me what had happened, he was laughing so hard. He thanked his guardian angel that Scott was with him as a witness. "I guess the bus driver is talking to his guardian angel, too," he sputtered.

Recording an Ambassador

There were moments of adventure so chilling that the adrenaline rush was electric. Through complicated circumstances, Frank found himself in a position to do a favor for the ambassador of a country that was in a whirl of political activity. We had become one of the "in" couples on his social list, and he entertained frequently and lavishly. He had also attended one of our large parties. Out of the blue, he called Frank and asked him to drive him to the airport to meet the foreign minister, and drive them back to the embassy. "I wonder if I should be suspicious about this," Frank said. "This is really strange. He says the minister might be interested in a program I'm putting together at the my corporate office." I was, as usual, jaundiced. When the Ambassador had been to our house, he always had a limousine with a driver and a bodyguard. It seemed to me that his request was too casual to be without meaning. But he had struck up a friendship with Frank, and they had indeed talked about Frank's new program. We decided to look upon this as just a lucky break.

This was almost too good to be true, as intelligence from that area was vital. Frank's case officer was excited. He gave Frank a sensitive recording device to put in his briefcase and record the conversation between the two men, which they correctly assumed would be in their own language. The recording would then be translated by an expert and put into a report. Because this was so strange and had the potential to be highly explosive, Frank and I did a trial run the night before. We put the recorder in his briefcase, put the briefcase in the back of the car, and drove around the block, making conversation in a normal tone, and then a hushed tone. When we turned it on, we found that it had clearly picked up every word.

It was show time.

The two gentlemen sat in the back seat. The briefcase was sitting at their feet. The Ambassador picked up the briefcase and moved it away from their feet. Frank held his breath. They conversed animatedly in their own language, and then in a very quiet tone. The drive was not long, and after they arrived at the embassy, the Foreign Minister said he was tired and went to his room. Frank and the Ambassador sat down in the library to have a drink. Frank took out his cigarettes, lit one, and put the package on the table. The Ambassador did not smoke. He pointedly lifted the package of cigarettes a few inches from the table, and let it drop. He was obviously wondering if there was a recorder in the package. Frank's heart stopped. He managed to carry on a light conversation before taking his leave.

How could they not have suspected the briefcase? Why had he asked Frank to go to the airport? As it turned out, the foreign minister was indeed interested in a new program that Frank was offering through his cover company, and as time passed, he and Frank became friends. He was a guest in our home whenever he was in town, and, in one instance when he was returning from Belgium, he brought me an exquisite piece of lace. He was a very charming man.

Wasn't it odd that the U.S. Embassy had someone able to translate that country's exotic language, but told us there was nobody able to translate reports in Spanish? Actually, it wasn't. Odd.

The Sweeper

During our stay in Spain, it was necessary for us to have the house "swept." This did not refer to cleaning as we think of it; rather, it was a test to see if our house was "clean," meaning that it wasn't bugged. I thought this was ridiculous. There was never a time when anyone could have entered our house when there was nobody home, but still, I had to consent. Then I was told that there must not be anyone in the house while the "doctor" was there. His code name was Dr. John. Nobody knew his real name, and this was the kind of work he did all over Europe. (He also installed the microphone in our speakers.) There were particular rules that must be followed. First, the house had to be empty. Even the maid could not be home. No problem, I said, we'll just do it on her day off. No, that would not be possible because we had to fit this into the doctor's schedule.

At the time, a friend of mine was staying with us along with her two-year-old daughter, who on the day of the requisite sweeping was sick with a flu and fever. Adding to this, it was raining outside. How could I justify taking the child out at all? And how could I take the maid with us? This was not something I normally did. I ultimately had to make up a really bizarre story about our having arranged to meet friends at the park. In the rain. With a sick child. With the maid. A small parade.

There we all were in the park with only one stroller, two toddlers, and a pissed-off maid who sassily stated after a few minutes that she was going home. I couldn't stop her, considering the fact that our "friends" weren't at the park to meet us anyway. When we arrived back at the house, Dr. John had left with Frank. Our little guest was flushed and so sick that we had to call an actual doctor. When I look back on those early days, I am beyond even laughing about it. Luckily, my house guest was away all day with a Spanish admirer she had met, because I am sure she would have absolutely refused to take her daughter outdoors, as I should have done.

Recruiting Jim

During our stays in different countries, we met other Americans who were legitimately employed there, or had even opened their own businesses after having lived there for a long period of time. Almost always, they spoke the language very well and had numerous contacts with "the right kinds of people." One of those men, Jim, became a very close friend of ours in Madrid, and Frank felt that he would be invaluable as a source of information. When he was sure of this, he described Jim to his case officer. We had a party and invited both Jim and the case officer, so that they could become acquainted. The case officer agreed that Jim should be approached. After a thorough investigation, the case officer advised that Washington had approved the approach. In the event that Jim refused, it was decided that the case officer, under the umbrella of the embassy, would meet with Jim, and if Jim was agreeable, he would be turned over to Frank.

This is the way it was undertaken. The case officer met with Jim and presented the offer, suggesting that he think it over. Should he accept, he would then meet the intelligence officer with whom he would be working. The case officer then tore an American dollar bill in half, and gave one half to Jim. He told Jim that a liaison would be made with his "handling officer" at a particular coffee shop, at which time the officer would put his half of the same dollar bill on the table.

The morning of this arranged meeting, Frank suggested that I join him, because this was going to be a source of merriment for us, just to see Jim's face. Frank and I were sitting at the window table sipping coffee when Jim entered. When he saw us, he visibly blanched. We were delighted with the look on his slack face. Frank ebulliently called him to come over and join us. Jim nervously glanced around, and could hardly say no.

We started an inane conversation, while Jim darted looks around the shop and sipped nervously at a presented cup of fresh coffee. When Jim turned his head for a quick survey,

Frank dropped his half of the dollar bill on the table. When Jim turned back to us and saw the bill, his mouth fell open and his eyes widened. He looked at Frank, then at the bill, then at me, then at the bill, and said, "You son of a bitch!" and we all burst out laughing.

Jim worked with Frank for the remaining years we were in the country and was never paid a cent. In various countries, the handful of Americans that Frank found in this way were never paid, and never asked about money or any other kind of favor. I asked one of them why he did it, and he grinned and said, "Because it's fun." Cops and robbers. God bless America.

Maids and a Window View of the Spanish Way of Life

Having a live-in maid was a clumsy situation for Americans trying to find the middle ground of firmness and kindness. My priority was always the care of the children and with good luck, we had maids who were like big sisters. That was why I preferred that a maid be young. A cheerful and caring babysitter was what we needed. With our busy social schedule, I was away from the house a lot of the time.

Madrid was a very social city, a late-night city, and Frank and I were night people. There were numerous expatriates from everywhere, and having been invited into a group of say, the Swedish "beautiful people," and the British contingent, we were considered to be social assets, and we commingled. Eventually, we belonged. We liked to mix and match people of various backgrounds, and in this way our social sphere expanded and our calendar was always full.

Spanish señoras were impersonal and autocratic and demanding with their servants. Our maid ate with the children, and their easy chatter from the kitchen was like listening to a second mother, calmly telling them to "be quiet and eat." It was less difficult for me to communicate once I was truly comfortable in Spanish, and didn't have to search for the tactful word to say. I think we Americans were actually scared of the maids, and I also think that the maids enjoyed it. To most American families, the idea of having a live-in maid was such a luxurious dream that we were primarily uncomfortable. A few American women had had cleaning women in the United States and were accustomed to preparing their lunch, and even having the food they liked on hand. Some women sat down and had lunch with the cleaning woman. (A señora would snort with laughter if told this.) It was not the American way to give orders, even gently, but it was definitely the Spanish way, and in our discomfort, we made Spanish maids confused, at the very least, and embarrassed and snide, at worst.

I witnessed the way Spanish women treated their maids, and in some cases I considered it to be downright rude and dictatorial. They addressed the maid with a wave of the hand, and seldom ever looked at her. The maid knew her boundaries and never talked back. A maid in Spain knows the drill and her place, which is in the kitchen or in her room. This style just wasn't American. We had freed the slaves.

Somewhere down the middle there had to be a compromise. Mine was to be firm, friendly, and fair. Most of the time that didn't work. Where to draw the boundary lines was always prickly. Spanish maids knew about the silly American women and they knew how to manipulate us. They preferred to work for us because they knew they could walk all over us. Gossip over the back fence with the maid next door revealed what she thought of us, and this was abundantly clear after I understood Spanish a great deal better than the maid realized. (I knew, for example, that *la bruja* meant the witch. Me.)

Over the period of seven years, a veritable parade of maids flounced through our portals and out of them. Once we hired a maid, Vicenta, who hated children but failed to mention that to me. She came recommended by an English friend who had no children. My friend also neglected to tell me that Vicenta was, as they say, a few bricks short of a load. The children told me that when she was ironing the towels, she shut her door on the third floor so the children wouldn't bother her, and that she didn't want to hear their shrieks of pain if they fell off the swing. One evening, when we were entertaining over cocktails in the living room, Vicenta marched through the kitchen door carrying a ladder and placed it in the middle of the dining room, which was open to the living room. She then climbed the ladder and began scrubbing the ceiling.

On the recommendation of a couple who were active in the theater, I hired a maid who, it turned out, was an alcoholic, a failed actress in her middle years, and who did not have any idea how to make a bed. I should have been suspicious when she arrived in a moth-eaten rabbit coat, her mouth a slash of crimson. Gloria Swanson had arrived. After three days of smelling liquor on her breath (our liquor), I took her aside to terminate her employment, and the drama began. I didn't bother to point out that she had done no cleaning. With wrist to forehead, weeping, wailing, she said she would not be turned out into the street and would lock herself in our attic. This she did. Our attic was an adjunct to the third floor, very hot and dusty, and the roof sloped in such a way that it was impossible to stand erect, but there she stayed.

I phoned the couple that had sent her to me and asked them to come over and reason with her. When they arrived, they said they didn't really know anything about her. She had been at a rehearsal and had said she was destitute and that yes, she would work as a maid. Now, I suppose, she was a hostage by her own choice.

We sat in the living room, whispering for some reason, and someone suggested dynamite. It was such a pathetic situation, but that got us laughing and we couldn't stop. We ultimately asked a Spanish friend, a courtly gentleman, to reason with her, talking through the locked door. When she agreed to come out to talk, her speech was slurred; she had settled in with a bottle of rum. I said she could keep the rum and she put on her rabbit coat and lurched out. Frank did give her a healthy sum of money to face the world without fear.

We had a very dear maid, Raquel, who loved our children and liked us. She was smart, literate, and capable. She left us only because her fiancé was called into the army. We had met him and found him to be worthy of Raquel. We were also invited to her wedding in the pueblo. When we entered the small pueblo in our black station wagon, we were hailed by the local denizens, waving at us from the street. They had never seen a station wagon before. The hospitality of Raquel's family, her cousins, uncles, and neighbors, was overwhelming. Her family's home had a dirt floor, and rabbits and chickens hopped in and out, enchanting our children. The night before the wedding, we were taken to a local bodega to drink wine without labels and watch the only television (black and white) in town. Outside the local church the next day, there were groups of people on the street to see the bride, or so we thought. Apparently, they were there to see us and our blond children. Frank made an extra trip to pick up the bride and transport her in his splendid, dusty station wagon. During the ceremony, people wandered in and out of the church, standing at the back and chatting.

After the wedding, there was a supper in the home of the

bride. Our family was placed near the bride at the table, which we considered an honor. We didn't realize that it was a prudent plan, because Raquel planned on serving us herself, holding her bridal veil behind her. We instantly protested, and it was with considerable force that we convinced her to take the honored place at the head of the table.

The entrée was roast rabbit, which I did not identify until Frank whispered in my ear. I hastily whispered to him that it would be unwise to tell the children, as the previous evening they had been playing with the rabbits. The wedding was a high point in our stay in Spain. We felt so honored to have been included in such a wonderful family celebration.

Ellen, a friend of ours from the United States, had a maid who was extremely outspoken and strident, driving Ellen out of her mind. "Maid stories" were a constant source of laughter, fear, or frustration. This was the culture shock that affected us the most. Ellen told me her husband had returned from a business trip to Paris, and had bought her a handmade silk blouse with a delicate collar of exquisite lace that tied at the front. When Ellen put it on top of the bed, her maid walked in, picked up the lace collar, and said, "Y esta trapo, que es?" (And this rag, what is it?) This kind of comment was not unusual. Unsolicited, frank opinions from maids were common. But not to Spanish señoras.

Maids were a large part of the Spanish way of life, and their service was awkward for me and other American women. We didn't have the finesse to handle them. It was a basic cultural difference between Americans and Spaniards. Our creed that everyone is created equal would make the Spanish laugh. We just didn't have the hauteur required to stamp on the floor like a dancer. And this applied in other circumstances, too; it was absent in all our dealings in the marketplace, the hairdresser, or a waiter in a restaurant. We just didn't get it.

Piropos

During the years we lived in Madrid, feminism had not been an issue anywhere, which was a blessing for the workmen on the street, who always showed their appreciation for a well-turned ankle, or any other feminine charm. This was something I thoroughly enjoyed. It was done with such good cheer, and without the sleazy aspect that is so despised now. Drivers of trucks would call out and construction workers would climb out of trenches in the street in appreciation of my unendurable and forbidden beauty. They didn't know that I understood what they said; my Scandinavian appearance was my disguise.

I remember a man holding a jackhammer, stopping the noise of it to say to me, as I passed, holding the hands of my small children, "Ay yi yi, leave your little brothers and sisters and run away with me!" How could one not laugh at such a ridiculous and inventive compliment? The calls and whistles I heard when walking down the street never seemed lewd. When we returned to the United States on vacation, I missed the voices of appreciation as I passed.

These men are called *piropos*, the literal translation of which is "flatterers." Was there anything wrong with that? I didn't think so.

Taxis

Two or three days after we arrived in Madrid, Frank and I decided to go out and explore the city. Taxis were plentiful. Frank put two fingers in his mouth and whistled for one as it passed us. The driver turned around and drove back to the corner where we were standing. He rolled down the window and calmly said, "No soy perro, Señor." (I am not a dog, Sir,) and with that, he drove away. This was our introduction to Spanish pride. An admired trait, most of the time.

When we had been in Madrid for some years, I received a call one Sunday evening from the maid of very close friends of ours. She was weeping. She told me that their baby had just died and became hysterical. I did not pursue details. I immediately threw some things into a bag and ran out the door and down the street to find a taxi. It was a quiet evening and I could see no taxis. I ran for several blocks when I saw a group of black cars, what taxis looked like in Spain, parked outside a coffee shop. I ran inside. A group of men, the drivers, were standing in a row at the bar with their espressos.

I spoke Spanish well by then so I approached the first man in the row. I told him that this was an emergency and explained that a friend's child had just died, but he demurred, saying he had just ordered his coffee. I pleaded with him, grabbing him by the arm and leading him outside. He shrugged his shoulders and got into the driver's seat, I rushed into the back seat. I was very emotional, so terrible was this news. I directed him to take a short cut that I knew would be faster. When we arrived at the apartment building, I looked toward the meter, and realized there was none. Confused, I asked him what the fare would usually cost. He turned around to look at me and said, "No sé, Señora, porque no soy taxista." (I don't know, Madam, because I'm not a taxi driver.) The Spanish were an extraordinarily kind people.

The Oh-My-God Adventure

After a few years in Spain, our family was allowed a six-week leave in the United States. We looked forward to it with particular enthusiasm because we were going to fly out of Madrid on the first TWA jumbo jet in Spain. The flight was headed to JFK Airport in New York. From there, we were to transfer to another airplane to visit my sister's home in Canada. Upon entering the plane, we were dazzled by its enormousness, as was everyone else. All of us passengers gasped, "Oh, my God." We were in a festive mood, as though in the midst of a cocktail party. After we were airborne, people wandered the aisles, carrying drinks, and stopping to chat. It was a celebration.

Seated a few aisles in front of us were a few Spanish soldiers who were going to an army base in Texas. They spoke no English. Behind us was a man from New York City who said he was a homicide detective. Both Frank and John were interested in his conversation. Seated across the aisle by a window was a beautiful young couple from Sweden, luminous in their glow of having just been married. During the flight, they had eyes only for each other, and they nuzzled and touched and whispered and smiled. It would seem that this is a description from the movie *Airplane!*, but it is true.

The flight was going by quickly, and the celebratory mood endured through the dinner hour. Frank had asked the stewardess about buying a bottle of duty-free scotch, and she said she was sold out, except for miniature bottles, so we bought them. Some would be given as a novelty gift to my sister. As we entered the skies over the United States, Frank noticed that the flight attendants were hurrying down the aisles, looking serious and intense. (As a pilot himself, Frank had a built-in antenna.) He knew what was happening. "I think you'd better get the kids ready to leave the plane," he said. I asked what was happening and he replied, "I can hear the carbon dioxide. We're going to have to do a crash landing. Now."

Frank turned to John and told him to remain calm and to get ready to go to the door of the plane as soon as we landed.

He told him to go in front of me. Then he told me to carry Johanna in my arms and Kristin on my back to go down the exit chute. As he was speaking, the stewardess rushed down the aisle, saying to everyone, "We are going to land at the airport, but we have an engine on fire so you must prepare to evacuate the plane. We will land safely and then you must exit through the chute and run away from the plane as fast as you can."

The plane landed with some bumps and then quickly hit the brakes, sliding to a very fast stop. We could hear sirens approaching. Outside the window, a fire truck was already spraying at the burning engine. There was an instant clamor toward the doors. The Spanish soldiers who had enjoyed a chat with John in Spanish were panicked, pushing toward the door, knocking people out of the way, including John who was right in front of me. The homicide detective scrambled to the aisle, pushing people down as he fled. I made my way to the door, Johanna in my arms, Kristin holding my hand behind me. An elderly man was waiting there, having been helped by the stewardess. He was ashen.

The stewardesses had opened the door but couldn't get the chute to open. After several attempts, they told us to hang on to the fabric of the chute as we slid down. The elderly man fell to the floor suddenly, I thought of a heart attack, but he had been pushed out of the way by the Swedish bridegroom. We looked out into the black of night and prepared to make our move. John took a step forward and crossed himself. Just as I turned to look for Frank, the stewardess came running down the aisle and said the plane was now safe. To stay, to stay! She told us we could wait on the plane until a bus arrived to pick us up. A truck would also arrive with stairs to reach the door.

I was very proud of our family, and especially Frank, particularly after witnessing the cowardly behavior of the other passengers. All of those who had pushed their way out had actually plunged to the ground, many of them injured. Good. Those who were left behind were in a state of shock. Some had never even left their seats to reach the aisle. When we looked at each other's stunned faces, some with tears, some paralyzed with fear, we knew we had to do something.

Frank divided the scotch bottles and he and I walked down the aisles offering scotch. The stewardesses retrieved additional small bottles from the kitchen and did the same. John and Kristin were sitting together and Frank was standing in the aisle, now holding Johanna in his arms. The pilot and co-pilot came walking down the aisle and we clapped, thanking them and offering them scotch.

A rosy nun walked up to join the group, took and tossed back her scotch with gusto, and accepted another. One passenger who politely refused a drink was the Swedish bride whose husband had just deserted her. She was staring out the window silently, the tears sliding down her face. I told the nun about the groom and she sat beside the young woman, holding her hand. It began to rain.

Frank was rocking Johanna and started singing a song the family knew well from a reel-to-reel music compilation that we played nightly during our cocktail hour. "Raindrops keep fallin' on my head," he sang, smiling at her face. Johanna's eyes lit up with recognition and she smiled, watching her daddy sing. "And just like the guy whose feet are too big for his bed," Frank sang as Johanna started to sing along to the familiar sound, even though she didn't speak English, ". . . nothin' seems to fit." Then everyone else started joining in: the stewardesses, the pilot, the co-pilot, other passengers, myself, and John and Kristin. "But, I'm never gonna stop the rain by complainin', 'cause I'm free, nothin's worrying me."

The truck with the stairs arrived along with the bus, and we made our way down the stairs and onto the bus. The bus drove us to a hotel. Everyone was strangely quiet. We were all so tired and shaken. We had no luggage, but I don't remember thinking about that. Despite the fatigue, I was too stressed to think about sleep.

When we were in our hotel room, the children turned on the television. It was the middle of the night and there was no programming. On the screen was an American flag, and then we heard the sound of the "Star Spangled Banner." I broke down into tears. We were home.

The emergency landing was front-page headlines in the *New York Times* the next day. We read that the detective had suffered a broken leg and that almost all of the others who had jumped from the door were also seriously hurt. TWA had arranged for our luggage to be forwarded to my sister's address. We never received anything further from TWA, not a letter, nothing. That disappointed us. (Frank wanted to have that scotch replaced.)

When John returned to school that fall, the class was asked to write an essay about the best time they had during their summer vacation. John said it was the plane crash.

Summers in Spain

During our time in Spain, we made a number of car trips to other parts of the country. We fitted the back of our station wagon with a mattress for the children, so they could nap and look out the back window as we drove. Of course, a picnic lunch was also packed, as it was a long stretch between pueblos. Just as in the United States, barely had we pulled out of the driveway when the children started the chorus of "Can we eat now?" or "Are we there yet?" Frank described an automobile trip with three children as "the same as traveling third class on a train in Bulgaria." He was not a good sport.

In Spain, there are converted castles along the way called *paradores*, which means "state-owned hotels." It was always breathtaking to enter a *parador*. There was such splendor in the well-preserved atmosphere of a castle centuries old. The meals were wonderful. There was no long menu, and this very simplicity was like tasting the essence of Spain. The dining room was a veritable museum of priceless paintings on the walls, and the antique furniture was not just displayed, it was used. The bedrooms were equally dramatic and beautiful. This avenue of displaying the great history of Spain was so practical, yet so effective in helping us experience part of Spain's history.

Miraculously, this was the cheapest way to travel. One had to make reservations very early in the year to be able to enjoy the *paradores*, and to arrange one's trip around their locations. Frank and I used to go to Andalucía, in the south of Spain, whenever he had business there. The Spanish accent there was almost unintelligible to us, just as in the United States, where southerners drawl. We were always entertained in grand fashion by the Spanish friends we had in the south. Lunch began at 2:00 p.m. and it was not unusual for it to go on until 4:00. Then we'd join them again at 9:00 p.m. for cocktails and dinner. When did these people work? In the south of Spain, it didn't really matter. The agenda there was to move slowly, speak slowly, eat slowly, and nap a lot. In fact, Frank sometimes wouldn't make concrete business appointments. He used business as an excuse to be there.

During the month of August, Madrid was closed. Business-men, bakeries, butchers, cobblers, and hairdressers put a sign on the door and pulled the curtains and headed to the beach to escape the heat. This, of course, was inconvenient for people who had to stay in Madrid to do business with Americans or other foreigners. In New York, it is Woody Allen's lament that all psychiatrists go to the Hamptons in August, but in Spain, everybody goes away. The premise is simple: it is too hot to work. It was a disappointing discovery for tourists whose vacations were during the summer months, but I'm sure the Spaniards didn't care. Life is to be enjoyed. Business can be carried on *mañana*.

We were only allowed home leave every two years, so in the interim years, we went to one of the coastal towns and rented a beach house. We ate at the outdoor cafés on the beach, with our bare feet in the sand, and the meals were simple, usually freshly caught fish with small potatoes, and a cold, local white wine. Even the children were given an inch of wine in proper wine glass, filled with soda. I don't remember ever being confronted by an inebriated Spaniard. Wine was an ingredient of civility. When John took his first Holy Communion at age five, the good nuns served the children a lunch and each child had a champagne glass with a splash of champagne in it. Of course. It was a celebration.

Sophisticated Children

We began a Sunday ritual, which was to take the children to dinner in different ethnic restaurants. We thought it would instill in them a cosmopolitan taste. There were, surprisingly, several restaurants to choose from: Chinese, Japanese, Mexican, Italian, and Hungarian, complete with violin. Our children enjoyed this adventure and other diners frequently complimented us on their deportment. This pleased us, because that was part of our plan, an introduction to the social graces. We had begun to anticipate that we would be transferred, as it was very unusual to have been in Madrid for seven years. As weeks and months went by, we were waiting. Could we be this happy some place else?

Would it be terribly hard for the children, now that they were young people and not toddlers? Had we made a mistake in enrolling John in an all-boys private school, entirely in Spanish? It had been his choice, but were we foolish not to look to the future and possibly British or American schools? Should we have enrolled them in King's College, so that they could become accustomed to English grammar? Frank and I still spoke in English to John and Kristin, but Johanna only spoke Spanish. None of the kids were accustomed to writing in English and they used Spanish grammatical structure, which resulted in a translated sentence like this, when John was talking about a friend: "You know that lady with hair blonde and eyes blue?"

I agonized that we had made a terrible mistake, although both Frank and I had beamed over John's school production of *Treasure Island*, with John playing the lead, confidently spouting his lines with Spanish gestures. There was a buzz in the audience when he appeared on the stage, because it was so obvious that this was not a Spanish boy. Frank and I were very proud, but had we done this for ourselves, to display our sophistication?

We were naive enough to think we might be sent to another country where we could use Spanish, but we were disabused of this optimistic outlook when Frank was told that his fine record with the Agency put him in a category where he would probably be required to take on a troubleshooting post where the situation would be sensitive. Frank was described as a "self-starter" and this qualified him to take over an office on his own. His case officers in Madrid had been completely supportive under all circumstances, consistently showing Frank respect and trust.

We were notified that the troubleshooting location was New Delhi, India. We were advised to begin to talk about an expected move, but we would have to bluff on this one, and say that we planned to move to Florence, Italy. Indeed this would be where Frank would have to train for six months, in a branch office of the new cover company. This, of course, also meant that we would be separated for that period of time. We couldn't take the children out of school until the end of term. We would immediately send the children to King's College where they would be privately tutored until the end of the school year, and would continue to attend English classes through the summer.

This was the way we told our story: Frank had met the executive director of an American firm at a dinner party some time before. They had had conversations on many occasions and the executive began to court Frank. He was very enthused about having Frank join his firm. At first, we didn't take it seriously, but ultimately the offer was so good, and so challenging, that Frank agreed to take the job.

Then, after the six-month training period in Florence, our story would be that Frank had done so well that he had been offered a managerial position in India, which he simply could not refuse. It would be a complicated web of lies, particularly because we would have to lie to the children as well. I hated that. This was a terrible way to live.

The Wiles of Women

I thought that perhaps a transfer might be a good change for us, as I had become increasingly anxious about our marriage.

We seemed to be drifting apart, and I felt that our entire social structure was too involved with Frank's hidden life. Frank had moved his own office to a suite apart from the large office downtown, because he felt that his frequent and sudden absences were being noticed. The small office was in a residential area, and only Frank, his (very attractive) secretary, and a Spanish employee were relocated there. The Spaniard was a retired military officer and a devoted friend named Carlos, who looked upon Frank as the son he never had. He came to our house every Sunday after Mass, to have coffee and chat.

After the office move, I noticed a distinct change in Carlos's attitude toward Frank. He seemed to me to be brusque and judgmental, like a disapproving father. When I asked Frank about it, he said that Carlos was such a straight-laced and proper gentleman that he was not happy about the change of office, and seemed suspicious of Frank's motives, making it obvious that he thought it improper. He had made his disapproval specifically clear to Frank's secretary, who was embarrassed by his attitude.

Carlos was at the office only three times a week, and Frank told me that he resented Carlos's attitude, considering it to be demeaning. I had to admit to myself that I shared misgivings, although I was more puzzled than suspicious, because Frank's secretary and her husband were also frequent guests at our home, as were their two sons. I felt strangely insecure. It was as though Frank's multi-charactered professional life had influenced his private life, and his sense of morality had been compromised.

I suspected everything, it seemed. The CIA should be comprised totally of women, because women can smell intrigue everywhere. We are natural detectives, predisposed to suspicion, as well as unwilling to stop probing until all the details are laid out. Women will briskly go through the contents of a wastebasket, pants' pockets, glove compartments, desk drawers, briefcases and even a hairbrush. They will study a telephone index for numbers with no names, or only initials. They will not hesitate to call a number, fully prepared to engage in conversation with the person who answers. Women can wing it. Women will study credit card bills and business calendars. They will examine the collars and even the underwear in the laundry hamper. They will smoothly pick up a telephone extension to listen to a call. There is nothing sacred when a woman is "on a mission." This does not necessarily apply only to CIA wives. It applies to all womankind (or at least, the smart women of my acquaintance). We stop at nothing. We will dig for details until our teeth itch. We want the pain. We will not be duped. We are born spies.

There were times when Frank didn't come home until very late, without a simple explanation, so I started to look at the entries in his business calendar. Suspicion became my business. Why were there so many entries to "Call P"? Who was that? We shared everything, I thought. Hmm, we had recently befriended a young, divorced woman whose name was Patricia. She'd come to our house, but I thought that Frank had responded with too much alacrity to her need for a ride home.

Frank was gone a long time. I asked him about it, my mouth dry. Mysteries were never to exist between us under difficult circumstances that only we understood. He breezily told me that he went up with Patricia to have a drink, and hadn't noticed the time. Two hours having drinks with a woman who doesn't drink? Once he said that he had stopped at the attractive neighborhood bar across from her apartment, but he forgot he had been wearing jeans (with no pockets) and a sweater, and didn't carry a wallet. Were the drinks free? Ice cold words. He said he had his credit card. I immediately made a mental note to scan the credit card bill. Another mental note to stop at the pretty little bar and ask them if they were open after midnight.

Deceit. Lying. Pretending. These were the fabrics of our everyday life. This is what we fed on. How unhealthy it was. On the evening of my birthday, when Frank was taking me to dinner at the finest restaurant in Madrid, he suggested that we stop to have a cocktail with Patricia. What? She was by no means a close friend of mine. Frank said he had met her on the street that afternoon. He was in high spirits, and her apartment was on the way. My teeth were clenched. When we came out of the elevator of Patricia's apartment building, she opened the door and we walked into her living room, a room full of my favorite people, shouting "Surprise!"

Frank and Patricia had been planning this party for a long time. He had specifically wanted the party in her apartment because I would have been suspicious about a party had we been stopping at the home of someone I was really close to. Patricia and Frank had arranged all the details, the catering, the flowers, and even a bartender.

I had once told Frank that I had never had a birthday party in my life, not even as a child. This was the first. I couldn't hug him hard enough, enforced, of course, by my feeling of shame. Patricia was an attentive hostess in spite of having a very bad cold. She and Frank laughingly told the room full of people that one day when they were coming from the caterers, they saw a mutual friend, and said, oops, people will talk!

What was I becoming? Was I going to be suspicious about every small incident in our life? That was our modus operandi, suspicion. Frank used to call me from the office every day, sometimes twice a day, just to talk, to see what I was doing.

And he most definitely called me if he was going to be out of the office, or late for dinner. There was no need for him to give me details. One night, when he hadn't called at all during the day and wasn't home by early evening, I began to worry. I waited. Midnight came and went and I was deeply distressed. I made a drink. Then another. Now I was scared. Was this an urgent circumstance that warranted my calling his case officer? This was only to be done under extreme circumstances, and there was a code phrase to use in the event that either of our phones were bugged. To make a phone call at 5:30 a.m. and keep it casual was pretty ridiculous. Fortunately, it was not unusual for us to call their number, because John had become a buddy of the case officer's son, and we'd become outwardly and understandably friendly with the parents. I phoned and used the code phrase, saying that I thought Frank might have been in an accident.

The case officer and his wife came over immediately. When they arrived, I made tea, and they both made light of my dilemma, with the glances that husbands and wives exchange when someone is being humored. Fine for them, I thought. They were protected by the embassy. Still Frank didn't come home. The sun came up, and they left. He said he would start making calls later in the day.

Frank was known for his courtly manner with the ladies, an engaging flirt, and was easily labeled a "ladies' man." I had never had reason to think he had ever pursued the women he flirted with, and the party flirtations never bothered me, except to be somewhat embarrassed by its constancy. Now I wondered.

At 6:30 a.m. Frank pulled into the driveway. I stood at the door in a sudden state of rage. How quickly anxiety and fear can change to anger. I wanted to punch him for not having been in an accident. His eyes were bloodshot and his clothes were rumpled. Why weren't his legs broken? He had been, he said, having a drink at the Hilton Hotel when he ran into a couple of Americans he had met in Washington, and they had "a few drinks" and then went to dinner, and after dinner they invited him to their suite for a nightcap, and he fell asleep in his chair.

How could he have gone through an entire evening and a day without calling me? I felt like hitting him, but I was too tired. I went to our bedroom and locked the door. But I didn't sleep. I worried about what the maid would think if Frank was sleeping on the sofa, or what the children would think. I felt used and betrayed. Now I was humiliated that I had called the case officer about something so embarrassing.

Much later, I heard that Frank was reputed, among his colleagues to be a problem drinker. Thus, the meaningful glances between the case officer and his wife. They had assumed that Frank had passed out somewhere. They were right. It seemed that all deep cover men were heavy drinkers.

The Tangled Web We Weave

It was going to be tricky explaining the radical change in Frank's workplace with a new company and an entirely different job description. We fabricated a story about the president of the new company having followed Frank's career. We said the monetary reward was too good to turn down. Frank would have to go to Italy for six months to train, which was true, and it was also true that the man in Italy who would be training Frank would actually believe he was going to be posted either in Florence or Geneva. The plot was thick.

I was not elated to be going to what was described as a

hardship post, meaning that we would receive a better housing allowance, and would be allowed to have "rest and recuperation" leave every six months, as well an annual leave. How terrible could this place be? I was not looking forward to six months on my own, never mind handling the complexities of the move, dealing with three embassies: the United States, Spain, and India.

What irony, that going to India to live should be so difficult. Who, in their right mind, would want to go at all? I had to go to the Indian Embassy several times, and I was constantly looking over my shoulder, because I did not want anyone I knew to see me entering or leaving.

The headmaster of King's College, long, lanky, needing dental work and a shoeshine, a perfect English man of letters, was "appalled" that we had been so crass as to send our children to Spanish schools since age three, but when they were given tests in math, geography, and history, they were found to be much further ahead than the British students, and they did well. We continued to pretend that we expected to be posted in Italy. We discussed telling the children the truth, but it was too complicated and confusing, so we decided we had to lie to them, too.

Frank made a secret trip to India to meet the man he would replace, as well as to check the housing situation. He was glowing in his description of the house we would inherit from the man in place. It had marble floors, five bedrooms and six bathrooms, a huge garden, a gracious veranda, and eleven servants. That's what he said. Then he left for Florence.

When Frank and I were separated during the six months he lived in Italy and I lived in Spain, I became increasingly uncomfortable about the role I was always expected to play. This period of time was stretching my emotional and physical boundaries beyond a place I could handle. The children didn't need me. They were very attached to our maid, who truly loved them, and when she was giving them their evening meal, there was a constant sound of chatter and laughing. Their lives were filled with school and games with the children in the neighborhood. During the past seven years, Spanish had become their primary language (and it actually *was* Johanna's first language). They often went to a local movie with the maid, who became fast friends with Kristin, sharing a love of books.

There were few invitations for me to dinner parties, which under ordinary circumstances, when Frank was home, would be frequent. This hurt me deeply. I would occasionally have lunch with one of my friends, and hear about a party she and her husband had attended, with hosts that I considered to be good friends of mine. I felt a tinge of paranoia. Didn't they like me? Was it only Frank's grace that made us popular? Did the hostess think I would vamp her husband? The situation was hard to accept because when Frank and I gave a party, I was acutely aware of the loneliness of single women and I made sure they were invited. Vamping my husband was the last thing I would worry about, as I was so accustomed to Frank spreading his charm and wit around. I knew that it didn't lead anywhere beyond the front door.

I occupied myself by organizing dozens of boxes filled with hundreds of photographs, putting them in albums. I borrowed records from friends and made miles of reel-to-reel tape of Peggy Lee, the Mamas and Papas, Sinatra. The music from this enterprise ended up following us around the world, and always brought back memories, even to the children.

But the bed was cold at night. I missed the physical comfort, the sharing of small problems, the laughter that erupted from both of us when we were together. We exchanged all our thoughts, and spending the end of the day together was as entertaining to us as going to a party.

I thought of Frank in Italy, with wonderful meals and good wine and conversation. In later years, Frank often referred to that time as being bitterly lonely, missing his family, taking long walks to fill a Sunday afternoon, reading in his small room. It was a hard time for both of us, and I cringe to think of how snappish I could be when Frank phoned, because he sounded cheerful and happy, which was a false face to present to me. I did not demonstrate such courtesy.

Visas and Hotels

Going through the tap dance of obtaining visas in Frank's absence, I felt that I was prostituting myself by wooing the friendship of the silly Indian Ambassador, who was young and lived with a blonde bimbo in the very American part of the city. He had no ambassadorial functions that I was aware of. If I needed anything from the Indian Embassy, I had to call him at home and then he would come to work. They invited me to dinner on two occasions, and he struck me as being a superficial child, which worked to my advantage when I turned in visa applications, with nonmatching pictures and a forged signature on Frank's application.

I had the distinct impression that people were not exactly pounding on his door for visas, or anything else, but he bestowed importance and aggrandizement upon himself. He was The Ambassador. Top man. I treated him with due respect, flattered him, and oh, how easy it was to make him think I respected him. He told me that sometimes the issuing of visas was a slow procedure because they were very careful not to allow the CIA in. "The government is very worried about them," he said, and

I told him I could certainly understand that. He demonstrated his considerable power by "pushing the visas through." I had expected praise from Frank for my visa trick, but he said nothing, except that he would be annoyed if the visas were held up by my chicanery.

This wasn't the Frank I knew. That Frank would have laughed and congratulated me. The life we were living now was so unnatural. We both had our own private hills to climb and overcome. It wasn't a team effort. From the beginning, we had shared the anxiety and bewilderment that presented itself whenever we stumbled to the tune of the clowns, as we fondly called the Washington choreographers. I felt I deserved more credit for what I had accomplished and endured on my own. The original plan had been that Frank would return to Madrid, we would make the rounds of farewells, and go to India.

There was a deadline for our arrival in India, due to the fact that the wife of our predecessor had fallen into a deep depression there, and had become a recluse, dressed in *dhoti* (the humble rags of the lower castes). She had painted a spot on her forehead, and sat staring at the wall. She returned to the United States and was being treated for depression, and her husband was eager to take the children and join her. This story did not cheer me. It was hard to be optimistic, and if the Indian Ambassador was an example of the upper class, it augured badly.

I was always taken by surprise when I received frequent calls from the new cover company. I was not use to being comforted or helped, far less *asked* what hotel I would like to move to before the transfer, the cost being of no consequence. I knew we could expect a happy alliance with them. There were times when we did consider leaving the Agency for a real job with them, especially with the large bonuses with which Frank was rewarded, and could not keep. They were turned in to the CIA, and they disappeared.

During our stay in Spain, Frank had no objection or argument about his assignments or the agents he was to deal with. He always got along extremely well with the liaison from the embassy, and especially with his case officers. He loved his job. How many people do? He even loved the cover job, because he didn't have to worry about it after he was established and had some experience behind him. Training for a cover job created extreme pressure, but once trained, he strutted into the office with élan, pretending he knew what he was doing. He was a good actor. That was fun. Nobody was going to fire him.

I loved our life in Madrid, and to this day, I feel nostalgic about it, as do our grown children. Spain was their childhood. It was *futbol* on the streets with their Spanish friends, and Spanish movies on Sundays, and trips to the pueblo and summers on the Costa del Sol on the beach, and long car trips to the north of Spain on the border of France, and swimming lessons at our country club, and a house ringing with the sounds of parties, and First Communion in the tiny chapel with the nuns beaming over them, and the love of Luisa, our dear, intelligent maid/friend over many years. Spain was home.

When I moved into a hotel in Madrid with the children, awaiting Frank's arrival before making our way to India, I was overjoyed to see that we had two adjoining suites. One suite had a king bed, and the other had two double beds and a very comfortable cot. I wondered if this was a mistake. I had had a few chats with the man with the cover company, and I felt I should call him to see if there was a mistake. The phone rang, and it was him, calling to see if the rooms were satisfactory. I told him how overwhelmed I was, as I had reserved only two adjoining double rooms, and I had asked for a cot for the maid. Although the children would have been quite safe on their own, they so loved Luisa that I had decided to have her with us for a while longer. My caller said perhaps I might like to entertain my friends, that all I had to do was sign the checks for meals, and by all means, invite them over. Yes, indeed! It was a beautiful hotel with three restaurants, a large swimming pool, and excellent room service.

Looking at our barren house after the movers had left, my heart ached. I could see the outline of the paintings we had bought at the flea market, and the carpet in the dining room. The house had a hollow sound. It had been so filled with love; I hoped it was contained there. Then I received a call from Frank, telling me that the head office of the cover company, based in the middle of America, had said they wanted him to work there for about six weeks to become acquainted with the people he would be dealing with. This, of course, was a good plan, but it did mean that we would go with him and live in a hotel there.

We had seventeen suitcases. New clothes for at least a year for the children and varied goods I had been advised we would never find in India. Frank was already at the home office. He asked me to buy a washer, dryer, and refrigerator to ship, because the voltage was not available in the States. I didn't know if I had the energy to do that. But I did.

When we arrived in New York, I must have looked as haggard as I felt. The gruff customs man asked me what I had to declare, and I waved at the seventeen suitcases and said, "Everything." He looked at the children lined up behind me and waved me through. "I think you have your hands full," he said. The hotel we stayed in in the United States was in the suburbs of the city, quiet, for the sake of the children. Very quiet. The children didn't complain. One day John said, "Why didn't we just stay in the hotel at home? Daddy's always working, and there's nothing to do." He had called Madrid "home." It was no longer a foreign country.

Frank and I were not communicating well. It was my nature to handle unpleasant situations by plunging into them and ridding myself of the feelings of foreboding and dread by discussing it, thrashing through it. Waiting for weeks, especially in a situation where I was idle, deepened my apprehension, and the pricklier I became. Frank knew this and retaliated with silence, though I deeply wanted him to try to comfort me and empathize. Frank shrank from emotional discussions and chose stoicism instead, and that made me feel shut out and angry, creating a feeding frenzy of nerves. And because I was vocal about my feelings, I always felt that I was being the bad guy.

Finally, it was time to test the visas. We started our journey to India.

India (1972-1974)

Arriving in India

We arrived in India on July 17th at 10:00 a.m. Under our new sponsorship, we travelled first class, and our trip had been luxurious. We basked and ignored the effete Qantas steward's glowering at the children. When we landed in New Delhi, the airplane did not pull up to an airport building to disembark. As a matter of fact, Qantas landed far out on the tarmac and a stairway was wheeled up to the plane for us, as we were the only people leaving. I thought this to be rather strange. There we were on a tarmac, a distance, obviously, from the airline terminal, and all we could see were a couple of shacks or sheds.

We were directed toward those sheds, and were told that they were, in fact, the terminal. As soon as we stepped outside, we were assaulted by the heat and the smell. It overwhelmed us. "A sewer must have backed up," I said as we all placed our hands over our noses. I didn't realize that this was the smell of India.

We were greeted by our soon-departing American in place, Jack, who tried to facilitate the process of going through customs. Absolutely everything was unpacked and then thrown all over the place. The customs officer said he had to keep our new camera, a tape recorder and other small appliances "for further examination." Jack explained that that meant we would never see them again.

The heat was like a wall. Within seconds, our clothes were sticking to our skin and we were all parched with thirst. Jack warned us to wait until we got to the hotel to drink water. While the customs officers were pilfering, I looked around the airport. There were a lot of ragged children standing at the exit begging, their huge black eyes dancing. The smell of body odor in that small confined space was sour. My legs had swollen in the plane and I had to remove my shoes, reluctantly, because I could see how dirty the floor was. I felt as though we had landed in hell.

We were in the building more than an hour. When we left and entered the car, the air conditioning was heaven. Our driver, Sharma, flashed his dazzling smile of welcome when Jack introduced us. I liked him. Jack told us that he would act as bodyguard for us whenever we left the car. "We need a body guard?!" I asked, stunned. "Well," Jack said, "you'll have 24-hour guards at the house, but the driver will go with you when you shop. He also guards the car."

I had expected less-than-immaculate surroundings, but had never thought any of us would be in danger. Looking out the window on the drive to the hotel, I was stupefied by the panorama of dirt shacks and the overwhelming numbers of people, and my reaction was that even the people looked dusty, draped in rags. The Indian children craned their necks, staring, smiling. I tried to persuade myself that most airports everywhere seem to be located in bad parts of the city, and the drive into the city is usually disappointing, but doesn't reflect the city itself. That's what I told myself. None of us spoke, except Frank, who was sitting with the driver, chatting. Frank could handle anything.

When we arrived at the hotel, we gasped upon walking through the revolving door into the lobby. I had never seen such grandeur. A gorgeous carpet, chandeliers sparkling like gems, brass fixtures and lamps polished to such a sheen that they resembled gold, personnel wearing such finery one would think they were royalty. The women wore saris laced with shining thread, and the men were in crimson uniforms trimmed with braid along with turbans of the finest silk.

We were shown to our suite, which was grand with a huge living room decorated in exquisite taste. The sofas and chairs were covered with raw silk and the coral carpeting led to a full dining room with hand-carved rosewood furniture, highly polished. There was a small kitchen, with a refrigerator filled with juices and cold drinks, which we were about to attack, when I saw that we had a wet bar with a faucet that had a sign: Potable. I gathered this meant the water was safe, and I thought it would be better than sweet drinks because we were rasping with thirst. Such naiveté.

The ambience of this astonishing setting was such a contrast to what we had seen and experienced in the last few hours. I suppose I should have felt guilty, but I felt enormous relief and gratitude, divorced from the smells and sights that no one could be prepared for. The contrast was shocking. We drank glass after glass of water, walking around the suite with our glasses, making approving sounds when we saw the bedrooms. The bedspreads were made of silk, as were the curtains.

Although we were jet-lagged, we were too excited to sleep and the children were eager to see a monkey park that I had heard about. We went down to the lobby and were swept out of the hotel by a gleaming doorman, resplendent in his finery. Not only were the hotel people opulent in dress, they were remarkably handsome.

As I looked out of the car window, my impression was that the city of New Delhi seemed like a small town with a population of a million. Women's saris were sepia with dirt, as they carried baskets or urns on their heads, gliding like models, and flashing their white smiles as we passed. They were beautiful. There were also beggars everywhere. I asked Sharma about the dirt houses and he said they were made of cow dung. He added that cow dung was also used as cooking fuel. Thus, the smell of India; and thus, the sacred cow.

As we neared the park, we were startled by a young man on a motorcycle, who tore past us without caution, and in an instant, a truck hit him, head on. He flew through the air and landed on his head with a sound like a crack. The truck drove away. The boy's body was limp. People on the street looked at him but did nothing. I asked Sharma if we should see if we could help the boy. "No, Memsahib, he dead, I think." He smiled. My God, did life have no price here? I had learned an early lesson. We were all so upset that we decided to return to the hotel.

As we entered the lobby, there was some kind of drama taking place. Hotel employees were carrying the body of a man in a bathing suit away from the pool. I could see blood seeping out of his ear. Someone asked if our car could take him to the hospital, since it was right out front. This seemed to me to be unwise, taking that responsibility, and I said I thought it would be better to call an ambulance. The hotel clerk informed us that New Delhi had no ambulance, so Frank immediately offered our car.

As I saw the car drive off, with the man's feet sticking out the window, I told myself this whole day had to have been a bad dream. No ambulance? It just could not be real. (The injured man had dived into the shallow end of the pool and suffered massive head injuries.) When we returned to our suite, Johanna, who was seven years old, asked in a whisper, "Are we going to see dead people every day here?" That was indeed a profound question, but I didn't know it at the time.

As though we all had been given a cue, we quickly found ourselves in terrible intestinal distress, doubled up with sharp cramps. Frank was spared, as he had not drunk the water. I didn't realize that this type of dysentery was a full-time companion, but I did know it had come from the water, and that we would not drink any more, not even, we were warned, to brush our teeth. I thought they should change the sign from Potable to Diarrhea.

By evening, I was loath to leave the children, but Jack had arrived to take Frank and me to dinner in the hotel, so I wouldn't be far away. Jack was a very personable man, obviously capable and well acquainted with the problems we would encounter. Amoebic dysentery was something that absolutely everyone suffered from, including the Indian people.

Halfway through dinner, I felt the urgency to leave. The cramps I was feeling reminded me of labor pains. My legs were still very swollen, and I had had to remove my shoes at the dinner table. Jack immediately understood that I had to return to our room, so Frank took me to the elevator. Before the elevator arrived, I fainted in a heap on the floor.

Frank managed to lead my staggering legs to our suite. I was trying to be casual about a mere attack of what was called Delhi Belly, and urged Frank to go back to join Jack. He didn't object. When I saw the children, I felt very guilty about having left them, and I was hurt that Frank had not refused to leave me. I was equally annoyed with myself for being such a martyr. The children were my responsibility. Weren't they?

John's temperature climbed so high that it was beyond the mercury level on the thermometer. He was delirious. I got a shower cap and filled it with ice and tried to cool his thrashing body while I knelt on the floor beside his bed. I realized that both the girls were also sick, but not as seriously as John. They were doubled up and asking me to help them to the bathroom. I should have called a doctor, but I did not realize how serious this condition could be. After a while, I did call the hotel doctor. He prescribed medication.

The next day, Sharma, my guide and protector, took us to see our house, which we were inheriting from Jack. The glowing description that Frank had given me was more than just a tad overblown. The floors were of green-and-gray speckled cement, not marble, the living room was divided from the dining room by dingy makeshift curtains on a rod, the kitchen was a huge monstrosity, containing a gigantic concrete sink, and the "garden" was a sea of dirt without one plant.

There was no sign of "a woman's touch," which I attributed to the fact that it was essentially a bachelor pad. The entire house was filthy and all the walls needed paint. The most dramatic touch, which no one had told me about, was that India's main railroad literally ran through the back of our garden, pretty much on the hour, with half the passengers sitting on the train's roof, and hanging out the doors. Every run of the train was preceded with whistles and toots. Picturesque. I put my head down on the kitchen counter and cried, careful not to disturb the mystery Indian who was sleeping on the counter.

Frank had already signed the lease, but I didn't care. I didn't want to live there. No amount of paint and polish was going to stop the railroad. I felt we could break the lease because we had not been made privy to the noticeable existence of the train. At first Jack was puzzled. "Oh, you just get used to it," he said. I thought not, and said I wanted to go house hunting. Jack said he would introduce me to his general manager, R. J. Gupta, who would take me to see other houses the realtor had available.

On the next business day, Frank went to a travel agency and

said he wanted to book a one-way flight for five on the first plane to leave New Delhi two years hence, on July 17th. The travel agent was dumbfounded. "Really," she said, "and where do you want to go?" Frank said it didn't matter, but it had to be the first flight of the day. She said there was a Lufthansa flight which would, as currently scheduled, leave at 4:00 a.m. that day; it would be flying to Frankfurt. "Fine," Frank said, "we'll be on it." And we were. Later, whenever Frank was asked how long we lived in India, he said, "Two years, four hours, and twenty-three minutes."

Our New Home

I began looking at other houses, and it seemed that those that were available were too small, too old, or not accessible. I didn't know the city at all, but later in my career I realized that R. J. Gupta had shown me houses he knew I wouldn't want, because he already had a deal made for a sizeable chunk of the money that would surely be paid for refurbishing the original house. I was naive in the ways of the world according to Gupta, in that most devious of countries. I succumbed, and began to arrange to redecorate. R. J. was more than enthused about hiring the necessary workmen. We remained in the hotel during this period and waited for the arrival of our furniture, which had been shipped by air.

Frank kept calling the moving company and was repeatedly told that the furniture had not arrived. His reason for concern was that the rains might damage the furniture, and so we wanted to ensure that it was properly stored. The last time he called, he was told the furniture had arrived, so he went to the airport to inspect the storage conditions.

The furniture was out on the tarmac and had been there

for some time, in the rain. Frank was infuriated. The moving company representative innocently pointed out that they had no room for our furniture, and he pointed to the sheds, which were full. Frank was a very tolerant man and hardly ever lost his temper, or even appeared vexed. He would eat cold soup in a restaurant rather than send it back and "cause a scene." When he looked at our antique Spanish dining table, and our beautiful Spanish carpets open to the air, he blew up. "I picked him up by the ass of his diapers and ran with him, heading for the wall, but I dropped him before his head hit," he said. Forever gracious.

I carefully monitored the work being done at the house, and it was a revelation. It was hard to tell the Indians from the ladders. Skinny bodies were hanging from the makeshift bamboo ladders, other skinny bodies were squatted all over the house sweeping with little bunches of what seemed to be straw. As I had instructed that the entire house be painted pure white, there could be no confusion. Painters were swaying from makeshift scaffolds. These people had apparently been hired by the dozen, doing whatever it was they were doing. Carpenters were building floor-to-ceiling teak bookshelves in the den, which we snobbishly called the library, a dream come true for bibliophiles like us. Books were treasures. A huge teak desk was made for Frank, and we suddenly could think of ourselves as the squire and his lady.

I was told that the squire's lady was responsible for the condition of the servants' quarters in the back of the garden. The quarters were humble, but were considered luxurious by most Indian workers. I did take these inspections seriously, more for the welfare of the servants than as a criticism by me. I did not care to inspect the communal toilet, however. The toilet was a big hole in the ground leading to a septic tank. There was a cold water tap there for "sanitation purposes." They did not use toilet paper.

Frank insisted that the furniture be delivered on the day our house was ready for moving-in. That day, a pair of water buffalo turned into our driveway with our furniture strapped on top. When we inspected the furniture and mattresses and saw the mildew, which had begun to sprout, we decided to unload on the driveway and yard, so the sun could dry whatever was salvageable. The mattresses were my main concern because they could not be replaced. After an hour or so had passed, I went out to look at the mattresses. I could not believe my eyes and ran to get Frank. Mushrooms were popping up from the mattresses, literally as we watched. It was impossible not to laugh. Frank said he was going to get his camera, forgetting we would have to call the customs man to take pictures.

The Shopping Trips

Frank traveled with Jack to familiarize himself with the factories and the people he would be working with in his corporate job. I stayed in the hotel and planned my shopping trips to buy curtains and light fixtures for the house. I told the driver that I had heard of a particular section, Old Delhi, where I might find the best brass fixtures. "No, no, Memsahib," Sharma said, "this is not place for Memsahib. Bad people. Bad thieves. Steal from Memsahib." That certainly was not going to bother me. I insisted that we go and Sharma shrugged and looked dismayed. Johanna said she wanted to come for the drive, and Sharma protested again. Reluctantly, he took us both, shaking his head with disapproval. When we parked the car, he said he would stay to protect the car, and that I must go in alone. He urged that Johanna stay with him, and I agreed.

I was immediately uneasy at the stares and strange laughter I was met with upon exiting the car. This was indeed a squalid area. A man on a bicycle, carrying long metal pipes on his shoulder, wheeled past me and as he turned, the pipes hit my neck and I fell into a narrow gutter, through which ran a stream of water and dirt. My skirt was wet. I don't know why I didn't go back to the car, but my pride wouldn't allow it, with all those eyes staring at me. It was important for me to feel that I could handle this country from the very start. So I marched steadily into the brass shop. I was advised later that I evoked stares partly because I was wearing a knee-length cotton skirt, and that my legs should have been covered.

I quickly chose three light fixtures and they took them into a back room to pack them. Would I like a Coca Cola while I waited? I accepted. I was very thirsty. They brought the drink in a glass, and I remembered the admonition: never to drink from a glass in a strange place. It was safer to drink from the bottle. I put the glass aside. I waited for a long time, shrinking away from my own clothing. Finally, I called to the back room and asked what was taking so long. I wanted to run away as fast as I could, but I stayed. At last they brought me a wrapped box, and I hurried to the car, feeling panicky. The car was surrounded by about a dozen Indians, their hands on the car's roof, all of them peering into the windows. A couple of children were there too, their faces pressed against the windows, snot sticking to the panes. They were shouting something. The driver was standing there and was not doing anything to dispel them. Johanna was in the back seat, eyes wide with fear. I managed to push my way through the bodies and squirmed into the back door with Sharma's help. Then they began to rock the car from one side to the other. Sharma got in the driver's seat, but made no effort to leave.

"Drive!" I demanded angrily. "Memsahib," he said, "maybe I kill somebody if I drive." The car was now rocking in bigger motions. I shouted at Sharma once again to start the car and drive. This was a nightmare. All the men were grinning through the windows with demonic smiles. Why was this happening? What reason could they have for taunting and frightening a woman and a child? Apparently, Sharma had known exactly what to expect, and made no effort to change destiny. "Start the damn car!" I shouted, "NOW!" When the car started, they did not move, but Sharma slowly inched it forward and they were reluctantly bumped away. I found it difficult to breathe and Johanna was shaking, trying not to cry. My anger stopped my tears. If this was an indication of what our life would be in India, I was terrified.

When we returned to the hotel, Sharma got the box out of the trunk and gave it to me. We hurried into the hotel and the elevator. As soon as we were in our suite, I tore off my disgusting clothes and stood under the shower for a long time. When Frank returned that evening, he cheerfully asked me what I had been doing during his absence. I told him I had bought some light fixtures. He asked where they were, and I told him the box was in the bedroom. He went into the bedroom, and moments later, we heard him scream.

A large, live rat had jumped out of the box! Frank was standing on the bed, horrified. (Rats in India can be as big as cats.) I called the front desk for help. Two bellboys arrived at the door, carrying a big rag to do I-don't-know-what with . . . to flail the rat to death, I suppose. It was discovered that the rat had made its way down the pipes of the bathroom, so they left in pursuit of it farther down the plumbing.

I never went into Old Delhi again. I was completely bewildered as to why this had happened. I did them no harm. Did they hate me because I was a foreigner? Was it because I wore a short skirt? Not only had the people on the street been hostile, wearing their sly smiles, but the owners of the brass store had done something unspeakable. Why was a rat packed in the box? Could it have been an accident?

My terrible apprehension began. It stayed with me always, sometimes expanding into cold fear, sometimes into revulsion. I did not understand this country, and I still don't. At a welcoming cocktail party Jack had given, we had met intelligent, educated, charming Indian people, and they just smiled at all of it. It was some kind of secret, an understanding I could not comprehend. The British wife of an Indian friend told me that she came to India as his bride, and when they invited numerous members of his family to meet her, her husband told her to hide her collection of perfume bottles, which were on the bathroom counter. "But these people are your family!" she protested. She did not put the bottles away. At the end of the party, the bottles were all gone. In her particular position, she thought it was their way of showing their disapproval of the mixed marriage, and then, quite honestly, she said it went further than that, as in the experience I had had. But she couldn't explain it. "This is India," she said.

At this point, she always wore a sari, and had learned to speak Hindi. She put up with no games. "But," she said with a smile, "I'm no longer trying to be noble. The cook does the shopping, and I hide even the toilet paper." And she laughed. I had also been warned not to go to the market for food, particularly meat, as most markets were in the open air, filled with flies, and one had to barter the price. For food? Having been warned that the cook would steal from me, I was undaunted . . . almost.

I told Sharma that I personally wanted to shop for meat:

mutton, beef, and chicken. Again, he protested vigorously, "Memsahib not like it." I was puffed up with independence and obstinance. For some reason, I was determined that I would not be made a fool of, and I would not show any nervousness. The meat market was set up in a dirt field, with newly slaughtered goats hanging from hooks and dripping blood. This was "mutton." They were beside roasts of water buffalo ("beef") equally bloody, fresh from the kill. I stifled my disgust to save my pride, ordering six mutton chops. A side of goat was given to an old man sitting in the dirt. He was dressed in rags, and had a large knife between his toes, which he used to slice off chops onto a page of newspaper, in which the chops were then wrapped. I had to admit a certain admiration for the art of slicing with one's toes. The man did have hands.

I scurried home, never to return. Let the cook cook the books. Everyone had advised, "Just let the cook steal 10%." I could live with that. As time passed, I realized that stealing or cheating was the norm. I don't think the Indian people took it seriously. It was a way of life. I had to learn this and accept it. I should not take it as a personal slight, and I should not allow it to anger me. I decided to give up my declaration of independence after this experience. I was depressed.

This was a hardship post, and for that reason we were contracted to spend only two years there. The heat was almost unbearable in the hot months of April and May, especially when we experienced frequent power failures lasting as long as 72 hours with no air conditioning, fans, or refrigeration. Of course, the stove could not be used either, requiring a good deal of imagination to put meals together. It meant that water could not be boiled, so we drank Coca Cola.

Finding New Friends

Every morning, I woke up with a heavy heart, wondering how I was going to spend the day. Some days I was more than just depressed. We were surrounded by poverty and pain, and the fact that I had a car and driver was not a luxury that meant anything to me. There were always problems to solve, and I didn't think of them as just challenges. It was more a case of just getting through the day. I had many acquaintances, but no real friends yet. New Delhi was a party town, as strange as that may seem, because there was no outlet for recreation apart from the community swimming pool, and a once-a-week movie shown at the embassy. Most of the movies were very old and dated, but we all attended, whether or not we had already seen Clark Gable in *Boom Town*.

We entertained often, blessed as we were with cooks and bearers and sweepers. There were a lot of garden parties in the evening, the ladies in their long gowns and the men wearing the uniform white shirts with short sleeves, which were made to measure at the "Blah Tailor." The bearer (butler) glided among the guests with his tray of drinks, and the irony of all this gracious living was that the liquor came from a bootlegger. This was our social life.

When we went to see the American International School, as it was called then, we were agreeably surprised. It was a well-appointed, fairly new building with modern, western decor. When we had an opportunity to talk to the teachers, we were also pleased. Some of the teachers were spouses of American Embassy people, and in the majority, they were truly dedicated (or they wouldn't be in India). There were extracurricular activities, as well as sports events which were enthusiastically attended by all adults . . . hey, this was entertainment.

John had never played baseball, and although he wasn't particularly interested, we thought it would be a good diversion. Frank arranged for someone in the U.S. to mail a baseball mitt to John. When we received a notice from the customs people, Frank went down to claim it, and was told there would be a fifty-dollar customs charge, which he paid. He just paid it. We were learning. John didn't take to the mitt, but fortunately, a British school in Delhi had a soccer team and we found out they didn't have enough players. John was overjoyed, they were overjoyed, and we were all overjoyed. We went to see his first games, and it appeared that Frank and I combined were the only fans in attendance.

It was hard for all three children, attending a new school. It was like auditioning for a role with all the odds stacked against you, and feeling that you would never get the part. Only time and patience could change it. There was a good drama class, with an excellent teacher, and it was an outlet for the girls to take part in a shared experience that would inevitably bring about friendship, or at least open the door. I was very pleased with the multicultural student body, every color, every race, every religion. Many of those children had similar backgrounds as our children, a majority of them being children of embassy personnel. They understood the heartbreak of moving.

Every embassy in the world seemed to be represented. For our children, it was like finding a huge box of chocolates, each one a different flavor, and the opportunity to find out which ones were their favorites. Unfortunately, they were not allowed to buy lunch in the cafeteria, because only children of embassy personnel were the chosen ones. I packed an enchanting lunch for them, which always consisted of chicken legs (scrawny) and Coca Cola. There was no sandwich, because we often didn't have bread. The kids told me later that they sometimes threw their lunches out the bus window and bartered for peanut butter on white bread from the Americans.

Delhi CIA

For the first time, Frank encountered a hostile case officer. We learned that the reason for this was that we were "living in luxury in a grand neighborhood with a car and a driver," as if we were being treated with special courtesies. We were simply living the life that a representative of our cover company would have. Jack had warned Frank that this attitude prevailed, but I would have gladly given up the driver and the bodyguards for one shopping spree at the American Commissary. It would be a luxury to get such rare things as bread and milk, or margarine, flour, sugar, or, the greatest gift of all: peanut butter.

The case officer chose not to personally meet with Frank. This, of course, was meant as a slight, but at least his emissary was amiable and apologetic. He was aware of the hostility demonstrated by the case officer because he had made it clear to him that under no circumstances was he to do any favors for us, stressing, as an example, that he would not be buying us a turkey for Christmas. The young man was embarrassed about this, especially as he and Frank became friends.

The emissary's wife was Johanna's teacher at the International School. She was a very engaging young woman and a good teacher. When she asked if I would be a "room mother" for the class, I readily said yes. A school-related festivity was coming up, so she asked if I would bake cookies for their little party. I told her there was no flour in the market, but if she could get me some, I would be glad to supply cookies. She said that would be no problem. Then she called me at home and asked me to drop in at the school to talk to her. When I did, she told me that her husband had told her she couldn't buy flour for me, and that they were both embarrassed by the situation, and truly sorry. I ended up buying cookies at the hotel bakery.

As for the turkey at Christmas? Diplomats from all foreign embassies had privileges at the U.S. Commissary. This included secretaries and clerks. I had befriended a secretary at the Australian High Commission, so she went to the commissary and bought a turkey for us for Christmas. She shared that holiday with us, and many holidays to come.

During the entire time we were in India, Frank never had a personal meeting with the head of the CIA there. We didn't even know what he looked like. We did learn that the U.S. Ambassador had been apprised of the presence of a deep cover CIA officer in New Delhi, and that he had made it known that he did not want to be advised who the man was, and there was only one. New Delhi was a gossipy small town, and all the expatriates socialized: businessmen, journalists, diplomats from foreign countries, but seldom members of the U.S. Embassy. We admired the Ambassador for his stand. He knew that if the deep cover man were picked up, he would be helpless. There was nothing he could do about it, leaving the deep cover agent in the hands of the Indian police, a circumstance we shuddered to imagine. And we did attend parties where we met the Ambassador on a very informal level. It was known that he liked non-diplomatic gatherings with real people talking frankly about real things. The journalists really liked him, describing him as a "no bullshit" guy and a rarity, gregarious and witty. Everyone liked him.

Servants

The fact that we had ten servants seems like unimaginable

decadence, but because of the caste system, housecleaning had to be divided between those who cleaned the floor and those who cleaned the furniture and made beds, those who handled food and served drinks, those who cooked, those who did the laundry, and those who looked after the children.

We had 24-hour guards at the front gate who carried machete knives. The knives were strapped across their chests and through their belts, and this absolutely delighted Frank. "Hey . . . guys with big knives at the gate. I love that." No one entered without passing the guards and being announced to me. Our gardener, who was called a *mahli*, gradually turned our half-acre of dirt into a colorful garden. (Frank once joked, "Isn't it interesting that our gardener has an Irish name?") The nanny, Theresa, was called the *ayah* and she was very dear to me. She was seventy years old and had previously been a nurse in the British Army. She was intelligent, kind, and fearless. She, too, carried a knife, which she tucked into her sari when she walked the children to the school bus. When their lives were threatened (a story still to come), she walked tall, ahead of the guards. She also stood guard at the kitchen door to make sure the kitchen help washed their hands with carbolic soap to kill germs, particularly if they had taken a "bathroom" break. Theresa was in charge of boiling the water for 45 minutes. She gave this order, to ensure that it would in fact be boiled for 20 minutes. It was difficult to avoid amoebic dysentery regardless of all the precautions we took. If a fly landed on the rim of a glass of lemonade, it was instantly contaminated.

It might be said that Theresa was my household spy. I truly loved her.

Initially, I thought the servants' quarters were bleak and bare, but I soon learned that multitudes of Indians lived on the street. Frank once called it "the world's biggest slumber party.

We had to harden ourselves to the constant barrage of beggars and the sights and smells of poverty everywhere.

When the car window was open, crippled babies would be pushed through, some maimed, some blind and with flies in their eyes. There were children everywhere who were called "spider boys," their arms and legs broken by their parents at birth in order to become professional beggars. I sometimes wondered why they were all boys, and was told that many Indian baby girls were thrown in the river, because they were "worthless." The life of a male child had value from the point of view of his ability to work and support his parents when his parents were old.

One particular spider boy could be found at the same intersection, every day. Frank passed him on his way to work. He was a beautiful child with huge, sparkling eyes and a dazzling smile. Every Friday, we gave him money. He knew our car, and always waved happily at us. He made me weep.

The scope of these tragedies was too vast for us to even try to make a noticeable difference, so Frank and I made a small contribution by paying for the servants' children's school tuition and uniforms. The driver's son qualified for university and we paid his entrance fee. The *ayah* had taken responsibility for her two grandsons who were in a private Catholic school. We paid their tuition and supplied them with clothes, blankets, books, and their transportation to and from school to spend the holidays with their grandmother.

We also looked after the health of the servants, insofar as it was possible. When Joseph, our bearer, told me his infant child was in the hospital and would die without penicillin (which was not provided by the hospital), I sent Sharma to the hospital to verify the story. It was true. Then I went to the chemist and bought the penicillin. ("Chemists" in New Delhi are not chemists. They just own a store and sell drugs.) Every day, I gave Joseph the daily requirement, which I kept in the refrigerator, and he would then go to the hospital on his bicycle. When I was told by Sharma that the child had died, Joseph had not come in to work, which I felt was understandable under the tragic circumstances. I sent Sharma to Joseph's quarters to see if he needed help, as he did not live in our quarters. When the driver returned, he said Joseph was drunk. He added that Joseph had sold the penicillin and had bought liquor. He was not absent because of his grief. He was just having a good time.

The next day, when Joseph came to the gate, I left instructions for the guards to turn him away. I was very angry. Joseph came back with his wife and asked for me. I went to the gate, fuelled with rage, and Joseph fell to the ground and crawled at my feet, groveling for his job. I called him a baby-killer. I wanted to beat him. Then his wife pleaded with me, speaking Hindi, with her hands together in the prayerful way. Did a mother place no value on the life of her infant son? Was his death insignificant? I would not let that be.

Our two guards were Nepalese. They slept in the servants' quarters and were always on duty when expected. We didn't know much about them until one, Lal, asked for time off to go to Nepal to see his wife and two children. He asked for two months off, because he was going to walk. We gave him the time off, and when he returned, I asked him, through the *ayah*, if he had been glad to see his family. He grinned broadly, absolutely beaming, He had been gone for three years, and he discovered he had four children now. His family had grown and he was a happy man. When I considered the variety of backgrounds and beliefs of the people living in the quarters, it was a broad lesson in cultures of different lands, religions, and lifestyle.

One night, when Frank was away on a business trip, I was awakened by a noise from the back garden near the servants' quarters. I peeked behind the curtains and saw the driver and the cook there, circling each other with knives. I called Theresa and asked her what was happening. She calmly explained that one was a Muslim and the other a Hindu, which was cause enough for a duel, but apparently they also didn't like each other personally. I sat ramrod straight on the edge of the bed, staring through the window in disbelief, hearing the sound of savagery. No one had told us that a household is more tranquil if the servants are of the same religion. Theresa was Catholic. Sharma was a Hindu, and our cook, Jimmy was a Muslim. In this case, Sharma had accused Jimmy of being a thief and their knives were unsheathed. Fortunately, they didn't advance on each other and were able to part without causing injury.

My dealing with Jimmy the cook and his weekly written report of rupees spent was a bumpy road. One week his ledger showed that he had purchased nine dozen oranges, which was interesting inasmuch as none of us had seen either fruit or juice. "Get out of the orange business," I told him. I was learning. The next week's ledger showed that he had bought several dozen eggs, but none of those had made their way to our table. I was disappointed that he was so dumb, but I didn't fire him. At least, not until a new scam was introduced.

I had been told about a pork butcher who had an actual indoor store, and who had learned to be a butcher in Canada. His shop was called the Pig Po. I went to see him and was very pleased with the clean condition and the quality of his meat. It was actually refrigerated. The butcher also spoke English well. I told the cook to buy pork, chicken, and eggs at this store, and to keep the receipts. It seemed for a while that the cook was following my rules, until one night when he served pork chops which were decidedly off. When Jimmy was putting platters on the table, I noticed he was wearing a new watch, which was an incredible luxury for a servant. He said it was a gift from his brother. Later in the evening, we all got sick.

One day Theresa told me that the butcher had phoned and wanted me to come to his shop. He told me that Jimmy had been buying bad meat from an inferior, dirty market, but had made a deal with the butcher's clerk, who would give Jimmy phony receipts for double the amount he was actually spending, and they split the profit. The butcher had fired his clerk.

I called Frank to come home to fire Jimmy. It was always better if Sahib dealt with male servants, and I had to admit, I found Jimmy menacing. Frank said, "Jesus, this guy has been poisoning us," and I agreed. "Well," he continued, "I'm going to wait for him in the library behind my desk, and you bring Jimmy in and I will be very stern and civilized, but I'm going to scare him and then I'm going to fire him."

I brought Jimmy to the door of the library, and as soon as Frank saw him, he leaped up and shouted, "You son of a bitch! You goddamned thief!" and he came roaring from behind his desk, as squires are wont to do, shouting profanities, and grabbed Jimmy by the collar of his shirt, and the belt of his pants, propelled him to the front door, and bump-ran him through the front door and through the front yard, with the intention of throwing him over the wall. But Jimmy was too big and the wall was too high. Frank, screaming, ordered Jimmy off the property immediately, called the guards to enforce it, and then returned, scarlet-faced, to the front door, where I was standing. "That was classy," I said. "I thought so," he replied. When we went back to the servants' quarters to ensure that Jimmy was gone, we found his room empty except for pictures drawn of the hammer and sickle. It was obviously a sign to scare us.

Most families had more than four servants, depending on the size of the house, and problems with the servants became a topic of conversation amongst all the bewildered expatriates. For instance, our friend Hans, who was manager of a large German company, arrived for dinner at our house in a hissy fit of exasperation, for which he was well known. "It iss sso miserable," was his favorite phrase. It seemed he had returned from the office after a bad day, and told the bearer he was going to take a bath, and wanted a martini in the bath. While he was soaking in the tub, the white-uniformed bearer knocked, entered with a martini on a silver tray, and threw the drink into the bath water. As requested.

An American woman who was married to a foreign diplomat, and who entertained with great style, told me about an evening when they entertained distinguished Spanish diplomats for dinner. She decided to serve suckling pig, which is indeed a splendid offering in Spain. She told the cook she wanted the pig to be beautifully presented on a platter at the table. She said she wanted an apple in the mouth, and snips of parsley in the ears. The cook said he could not do that, but she insisted. She also pointed out to the bearer that it was time he started passing platters through the dumb waiter (the window opening between kitchen and dining room), to save steps walking around the kitchen door and into the dining room. He also said no.

"I don't care what you think," she said impatiently, "that is the way I want it done!" On the evening of the dinner, when all the guests were seated at a meticulously set table, with the finest linen and crystal gleaming in the candlelight, she rang the bell for the bearer. One skinny brown leg came through the dumb waiter pass-through, then the bearer's rump appeared, then the other leg, trying to balance the platter as he attempted to wiggle into the dining room. She rushed over and had a whispered word with him. He henceforth came around the kitchen door.

When the first course had been served, they awaited the pièce de résistance, the entree. The cook pranced into the dining room, carrying the platter with the suckling pig. In the cook's mouth was a red apple, and in his ears were sprigs of parsley. Luckily, Spaniards have a great sense of fun. What a way to break the ice!

Corruption and a Hit Man

Frank had inherited what appeared to be a qualified, savvy staff at the corporate office, highly praised by Jack and well schooled in company dealings and rapport with the factory owners outside of New Delhi.

In the course of Frank's business days, more amazing schemes were revealed. It had been a while since Frank had received any replies to his correspondence to the United States office, and time was of the essence. He was frustrated by the fact that it was just about impossible to make a long-distance call from India. Then he received a call from his immediate superior in the U.S., who asked, "What is happening over there? We haven't had one report from you in weeks!" This was very odd. Frank told his very wise secretary about the call, and in a short while, she knocked on his door, and with hanging head, told Frank that she had been able to find out what had happened. The mail clerk, at the end of the day, went off on his bicycle to the post office, carrying the day's mail, but when he was far enough away from the office, he removed all the stamps from the envelopes and threw the mail away, thereafter selling the stamps. A small business enterprise.

It was impossible for Frank to keep tabs on all the oral agreements with the office, so R. J. Gupta usually travelled with him, to translate and write reports when the discussions were in Hindi. Without trust, it would have been impossible for Frank to delegate responsibility, and without such delegation, his wheels of industry would have ground to a halt. There was bad blood between Gupta and another middle-management employee, who suspected that Gupta was getting kickbacks, but had no proof. Then, one day, Gupta left his wallet in the men's washroom at the office, and his adversary went through his papers. The evidence was there. He had been embezzling funds for a long period of time, taking bribe money from factory owners and saying it was "for the American boss." This had been happening when Jack was there, and it was continuing. It was particularly nefarious that he was smearing the reputations of both Jack and Frank.

At the same time, Sharma revealed that Gupta had made an enormous amount of money during the period of our home renovation, demanding kickbacks from the tradesmen, and falsifying the numbers when the bills were turned in. Of course, Frank was outraged.

When the evidence proved solid on both fronts, Frank called Gupta into his office, charged him with taking bribes, and fired him. Gupta tried to persuade Frank to change his mind, ignoring the evidence. He then threatened Frank by saying that if any charges were brought against him, he would arrange to kill me and the children. Gupta said he could hire someone to kill the children for fifteen rupees, and added that he knew where the school bus stopped.

We knew we had to take extreme precautions. Frank had never planned to bring any charges against Gupta, as he was certainly not interested in revealing anything at all about the office, wanting to keep a low profile at all times. His CIA superiors agreed. We discussed having Sharma drive the children to school, and also pick them up, but realized that this was a short-term solution, as business had to be tended to as usual, and how long could we wrap the children in cotton? I was terrified.

An entire posse of our servants accompanied the children to and from the bus stop: the guard with his machete, the *ayah* with her knife, and the bearer as a lookout. "I have killed before," Theresa said quietly, "and I will kill again for my children." I was not allowed to go because I also had been threatened. My hatred for Gupta was lightning white. Frank had also suggested it would be a good idea to keep a shotgun in the car. Sharma had been a soldier in the war, so he owned a shotgun, and he feared nothing. Knives, however, seemed to be the weapons of choice in these exotic surroundings.

One Sunday morning, as we were lingering over our tea, the guard told us that our neighbor, D.J., had come to visit. He lived in a beautiful home, two doors down from ours, and we had been there when he entertained. He was a highly respected and wealthy businessman. We were puzzled that he had chosen to visit us on a Sunday morning, but we welcomed him at the door. He was accompanied by another man of very large proportions, unusual for an Indian, whom he introduced as his brother, Raman. As we were sipping tea, D.J. told us he had heard of Gupta's threat (Delhi was always abuzz with gossip) and that his brother, Raman, would be glad to kill Gupta for us.

Hearing this said to us, with the lilt of the Indian accent, was absolutely shocking. We were dumbstruck, realizing he was serious. He went on to say, in a very conversational way, that Raman had killed people before, and would be happy to do it as a favor for good friends and neighbors like us. I confess, without shame, to being very enthusiastic about this plan. In fact, if I had had pompoms, I would have jumped in the air and done the splits. I realized I was sitting on the edge of my chair, with eager anticipation to get it done.

Frank said he appreciated the thought, but he would decline this generous offer. Then D.J. said, "Would you like Raman to stay outside Gupta's house every morning? Raman is famous. People fear him." Once again, I nodded my head vigorously. Once, D.J. said, Raman had stayed outside of the house of the president of a soft drink company, when truckloads of Indians had been hired to throw rocks at the house and the family members. "Raman shot the sandals off one man and then the others decided to go away," he said gently.

The casualness of this conversation was like that of people discussing a sports event. It was civilized and light-hearted. Of course, Frank was shocked. (Those Catholic schools had done the trick.) He thanked D.J. for his neighborliness, and declined his offer. During the entire discussion, Raman sat, saying nothing, except for small grunts of approval when his brother spoke.

When they left, Frank looked at me with astonishment. "I just cannot believe that you were actually eager to do this! It's downright shocking!" I didn't think so at all. I sarcastically told him that I thought we could just follow along with the Indian customs, and at least we would fit in. At least let Raman shoot Gupta's sandals off, that would be nice (except that Gupta wore wing-tipped English shoes; he could afford them). Frank shook his head and said, "I don't think D.J. has spent much time following the teaching of Mahatma Gandhi. And neither have you!"

The Tryst

New Delhi was reputed to have more diplomats, and indeed more embassies, than any other city in the world. There were embassies from little countries we had never heard of, represented splendidly, for what purpose nobody knew. The political section of the CIA was amply represented.

Frank was the only deep cover CIA officer in India, to our knowledge. He was definitely the only one in Delhi. One of the agents Frank inherited was a highly placed official in the Indian government, who was privy to the most classified intelligence at the highest levels. His lofty ambition was nothing more than to get out of India and be appointed to a significant diplomatic post in the U.S. This had been promised to him by a high official in the CIA in Washington.

Frank valued his loyalty and admired him for the chances he took and for his ambition to make a difference. Ashok was in such a sensitive position that under no circumstance would we entertain him at dinner parties or any social gathering in our home, but we did invite him to dinner alone. Frank would pick him up in a different car, and Ashok would lie on the floor of the back seat, unseen by our guards at the gate. When Ashok had microfilm to turn over, he was extremely nervous, even carrying it out of his office. These films were incendiary information that were of such importance that Frank would copy them instantly and send them to Washington within hours. At one time, the information was sent directly to Henry Kissinger on an airplane somewhere over Southeast Asia.

Frank was told by the embassy that he should regularly meet Ashok at an apartment in the American Embassy housing units. This was an appalling idea. Only Americans were ever seen there, and there were guardhouses at both the entrance and the exit to the enclave. It was folly to expect that an Indian gentleman might drive in, unnoticed, and using his own key, enter an apartment. It was decided that Ashok would enter the apartment with me, and that I would have the key, although Frank would already be there. We would walk arm in arm and always carry a bottle of bootleg scotch, giving the impression that this was a lovers' tryst. This apartment was a safe house, used for meetings such as this, but the Indian guards would never have noticed. My face was not familiar there, except that I was very obviously an American, and I was sure I did not know anyone who lived there. We did this on a regular basis, and I always stayed until Frank had used the copy machine and conferred with Ashok, then Ashok and I would leave together. This was the only way he felt safe, and he and I got along well together.

Frank was told that a very important representative of the CIA would be visiting India just to see Ashok. He was the man who had recruited Ashok and promised him a job in Washington. But Frank was informed that he was going to renege on his promise, because he had decided Ashok was much too valuable where he was. We called this officer "Silver Tooth" because he had braces on his teeth, even though he was about forty years old. Frank was incensed when he heard that Ashok was going to be betrayed, and said he would not have anything to do with it. In fact, he would fight for Ashok's promised reward. He too had promised Ashok that he would do everything possible to ensure that Ashok got the posting he had been promised and deserved. Silver Tooth brushed this aside, saying, "It doesn't matter what you promised him. I'll just tell him he shouldn't pay any attention to what flunkeys have to say."

On the night Silver Tooth was coming to meet Ashok at the apartment, I was there, and Ashok was very nervous. I knew what was about to happen, but did not reveal this, except to vehemently urge him not to accept anything less than what had been promised. "But he is my mentor," Ashok said, "and my friend." How wrong he was, but I could not say more. Silver Tooth came in the door of the apartment, and looked at me with shock and obvious disapproval. He did not ask for an introduction, nor did I offer one, as it did not seem appropriate. I excused myself and left the apartment.

The next day, Silver Tooth demanded a command performance meeting with Frank. "Just who was that woman in the apartment? I demand an explanation and an apology!" Frank said he would not apologize, and the explanation was simple. Silver Tooth waved the Old School Tie and said that if he did not receive a written apology, and if Frank did not support the cancellation of Ashok's post in the United States, Frank would "wait a very, *very* long time for a promotion." Frank supported Ashok without wavering. All Ashok had to do was refuse to carry on with the CIA.

It was more than five years before Frank got a promotion. Until that time, he had been rewarded annually, and each time, his case officer voiced his personal appreciation. As Frank had no rapport whatsoever with the head of the CIA in India, there was no place to turn for support or justice.

Many years later, Silver Tooth's name and face became front page and television news. He was accused of inexcusable activity under the guise of the CIA. He had actually broken the law and could face a possible prison sentence. I was delighted. And sad. Frank was no longer here to enjoy his vindication.

The Gods Smile Down

Without a sense of humor, the daily hardship of living the

way we did would have been intolerable. When we awoke in the morning, Frank would pull up the window shade and cry, "Oh, look! Another sunny day!" This was during a siege of power outages that left us limp. My quasi-solution was for us to sleep on the green-and-gray speckled floor, wrapped in wet sheets that I'd swished through the bathtub. The sheets dried in twenty minutes. We were all eager for the monsoons to start, not knowing that sheets of rain would fall so heavy that visibility turns to zero, or that the temperature wouldn't drop one degree. When the downpour stopped, the ground would hiss and steam. During our first monsoon, we were at the American Club swimming pool, which subsequently closed for the summer because the heat of the water and its contamination could cause meningitis. Goody, one more disease to outwit. On the drive home, a downpour came that felt like the wrath of God, the water hitting the windshield as in a car wash, with no visibility. When we stepped out of the car, we were already ankle-deep in water.

The heavens opened up to display more than just monsoon rains. Our first dust storm was a force of nature that was truly awesome. We were sitting outdoors in our garden with Indian friends who said, "Uh-oh, better bring in the lawn furniture," as they pointed to the sky. A galloping vortex of orange dust was heading our way, and before we could make a move, it was upon us with such a passion that we could hardly stand erect. The chairs flew in all directions. This was not a flash storm. This storm meant business. Dust was in our teeth, our eyes, our mouths and nostrils, hitting us like a Mack truck.

It was still raging the next day. I had to go to the chemist to pick up my amoeba pills, and I wore a scarf tied tightly around my head, and another around the bottom of my face, like an old-time bandit. Pitting my head against the wind, and bending from the waist down as I faced the orange dust, I ran into one of John's teachers, a very fey friend of ours, who was bound and gagged with scarves as I was. We stopped briefly, with our arms around our heads, to chat. "Why aren't you in school?" I asked. "Well," he said, "I woke up this morning and looked out the window, and I said to myself . . . on a day like this, how can I be cooped up in a school room?" "I can understand that," I said, laughing. And we staggered to our cars.

Johnny Walker

In order to have a cocktail party or the drink one prayed for at the end of the day, we had to contact a bootlegger, who would deliver whisky wrapped in the ubiquitous newspaper, on a bicycle. Word of mouth passed information about how to contact a bootlegger, and Indian friends directed us to a newsstand which also sold contraband American cigarettes. We were impressed with the brilliance displayed by the people who sold "scotch."

We planned to give frequent parties during the Christmas season, and ordered a case of Johnny Walker. Bootleggers never seemed to have vodka or other selections, so everyone drank whisky. When we opened the first bottle, we could smell the kerosene, and a systematic opening of the others proved that we had a case of tea and kerosene. They had learned how to mix and bottle tea and kerosene, and then seal the bottle with a perfect Johnny Walker seal, unbroken. It was truly a work of art.

It was never the intention of the bootlegger that anyone should drink this concoction, because it was obvious, as soon as the top was off the bottle, that it contained kerosene. It was entirely in the presentation. It was the perfect color in the sealed bottle, and the perfect seal. And the fleet-footed bootlegger sailed down the street as fast as his skinny legs could pedal, long before we opened the first bottle. His quick flight was not odd, because bootlegging was against the law. Right?

We Speak Spanish Here

I joined a women's club composed of women who spoke Spanish, and we had luncheons by turn at each other's homes. During that period, we spoke only Spanish. For some, it was their native language, and for others, it was a language learned in another country. Those luncheons were a lot of fun, as though the flavor and vitality of Spain had followed us for a while. The women were wonderful and there was a great deal of laughter. There are some rich Spanish phrases, which cannot be as colorful when translated.

At one meeting, we discussed the possibility of having an evening dinner party so that our husbands could meet each other. This suggestion was met with enormous enthusiasm, and it was decided that we would cook as many Spanish or Mexican dishes as we could, with whatever ingredients we could find.

One of the group was an attractive American woman who had lived in Madrid for a few years because she had been engaged to marry a Spaniard when she was quite young, hence her study of the language. The engagement did not last, but her love of the language did. She had subsequently married an American diplomat. Turned out, he was the case officer who was hostile to Frank.

It was decided that because I had the largest living room and veranda, our house should be the location of the dinner party. There was one small potential problem: A woman from Spain, who was in our group, was married to an Indian who was an agent for the CIA, working for Frank. How could we invite "Bob" (our name for him), and the case officer, David, to the same party? Frank didn't think there would be a problem because David had only read reports from and about Bob, and didn't know who he was. Nor had Bob ever heard of David.

On the night of the party, we experienced a rare, chilly evening, which botched our plans for the party to move out to the veranda. David was not a party person, obviously. He wore a grim face. I saw that he had cornered Frank and they were having a serious discussion in the library, which opened to the veranda. Bob didn't handle liquor well, but he loved drinking and dancing and began twirling to the music, first in the living room, then out to the veranda, like Gene Kelly, and I was horrified to see him suddenly burst into the library, with a pirouette and a bow. Later, Frank told me that after the bow, he threw his arms up and said, "Here I am! The spy who came in from the cold!" I think David's wife should have waited for another Spaniard.

Delhi Belly and the Arsenic Pact

On the day I arrived, when I collapsed with dysentery, I had no idea how serious the invisible amoeba was. For some of us it was permanent, a full-time occupation. And for two people we knew, it was fatal. One was a sixteen-year old American boy, and the other was a man with the Australian High Commission. The amoeba had invaded his liver and ultimately, his heart. He had been sent back to Australia, where he died. A German woman, who was a friend of mine, had to return to Germany and was hospitalized for more than two months there.

This condition was not something that anyone laughed about, and we openly discussed the problem with each other.

120

Our "specimens" were sent to the pathologist on a regular basis, and depending on how vehemently the amoeba had taken over, the condition was graded with a number of Xs, much like a restaurant reviewer using the $ sign to grade the expense category. I had the dubious distinction of having five Xs on my report, and the even more dubious distinction of receiving a request from the pathologist to send her an extra specimen for her to show her students at the medical school, because "it was the first time the amoebas were almost visible." I was the champion.

Treatment of amoebic dysentery was a medication to be taken three times a day, if the situation was serious. The medication caused vertigo, headache, and nausea, as well as depression. It contained a small amount of arsenic. When my condition became even worse, the pain was intolerable and constant. It was the only pain I have experienced that was as bad as full labor pains. It was potentially embarrassing for me to go anywhere during a bad siege, and I had actually fainted in the bathroom, more than once, left so weak when I regained consciousness that I couldn't even crawl. I just hoped that someone would find me there.

My doctor told me that drastic measures had to be taken. He took a deep breath and then told me that he thought I should take ten tablets at one time. He knew it would be an awful assault on my body, but it was his opinion that primarily, it would be an assault on the amoeba. I immediately balked and asked if that amount of arsenic might actually kill me. The doctor, who had become a personal friend of ours, said he had given it a lot of thought, and that he had been apprehensive too, so he himself had taken ten tablets at once, in his home with his wife monitoring his reaction. "I survived," he said with a smile and a shrug. It was very courageous of him, not to mention altruistic. He did say that the resulting vertigo, disorientation, and abdominal pain were hard to take for at least twelve hours. Still, he was suggesting such drastic measures because he feared the amoeba might invade my liver or my heart.

The doctor had come to our house to talk about this, and had asked that Frank be there to help me to decide. Poison. A difficult decision, but ultimately the only one. Frank did something that I considered to be the epitome of gallantry and love. He insisted he would also take ten tablets, and stay home with me, even though his attacks of dysentery had always been mild. He said we would go through the day together. Frank had always been an attentive and romantic man, but there was nothing that he had ever done before or since that so displayed his unselfish love and generosity. It was our arsenic pact. It was a terrible twelve hours, but I didn't have to do it alone.

Hospitals

All foreign residents were regularly inoculated for cholera, small pox, typhoid, and sometimes tetanus. Everyone feared hepatitis; there was no inoculation for that. If we were exposed to it, early shots of gamma globulin were advised. The local hospital was fondly called the "hepatitis factory." If you didn't have it when you were admitted, you would have it when you left.

The fear of hepatitis was such that we couldn't pursue our collective hobby: drinking. Malaria was also a danger, especially during the monsoons when the mosquitoes seemed to rain from heaven. There were very few days when I felt well, so I tried to go on with whatever my normal life was. One evening when we had guests, I became very tired and was trying to ignore a terrible headache. Theresa came to the door of the living room and beckoned to me. I went out to the hall where she was waiting. "I think Madam look sick," she said, holding out a thermometer. She took my temperature, and it was dangerously high. Her suspicions were correct. I had malaria, but I hadn't noticed it because I was so accustomed to feeling awful.

Due to the loss of fluid in my body, I was constantly fatigued, and I had vitamin B12 and iron injections every week. Going to the clinic was a dreary experience. It was dark and dirty, and the room to which I was escorted usually had bloody rags on the floor or even on the examining table (where were they from . . . ?). I refused to even sit on the table, and always took my shots standing up. I was very wary about the doctor's repeated use of the same hypodermic needle, and I could see no sterilization. When I told the doctor about my concern, he said he could readily understand my misgivings, and said he wished disposable needles were available, not only for me, but for the clinic. I told him I would write to a friend of mine who was a doctor in Canada, and ask him to send a case of disposable syringes directly to my doctor, thus avoiding problems with customs. When the doctor went to pick up that box at customs, he discovered that every single needle had been snapped in half "to see what was in them."

Our doctor had gone to medical school in the United States, so we had confidence in his credentials, but bemoaned the shocking facilities available to him. One time Johanna had cut her finger; it had become swollen and it hurt. I could see the wound had become infected. The infection trailed in a red line from her finger up her arm, and I knew she had blood poisoning.

We were in the middle of a power outage but Sharma rushed us to the clinic, which was also experiencing the blackout. It was the dinner hour, and the air was dusty with the burning of cow dung, the Indian cooking fuel.

The doctor suggested he take Johanna out to the street to lacerate her finger. I was shocked, immediately turning into a witch as I pulled Johanna away from the doctor. I shouted, "We're going to the British American Hospital, and she is going to have a general anesthetic in a clean operating room!"

I knew that the British American Hospital had its own generator, and I knew that its facilities were not available to regular businessmen; only diplomats were admitted. The doctor reminded me that we did not have the right to use the British American Hospital, but I was on a rant. I couldn't possibly remember the stream of epithets I spat on the way about the horrors of that country, and if the doctor tried to say anything, I hissed.

Nobody tried to stop me from entering the hospital because I was unstoppable. Their generators were working and an operating room was available. My child was safe. I could not have been more terrifying if I had had a gun.

The Episode

One day we were visiting friends at their home for lunch, enjoying their imported American coffee. I began feeling unwell, which was not unusual, but this was a new sensation. I was weak and dizzy and short of breath, and then suddenly felt cold and strange, and fell to the floor unconscious. This was the second time that I had experienced these sensations. The first time had been a week before when I went to a movie with Indian friends. Frank was out of town, and I had appreciated their invitation. I felt a pain in my chest and arm, but ignored it as "just one more thing" for my medical chart. I didn't want to say anything to cause them to leave the movie.

On that Sunday afternoon of our coffee worship, Frank

thought, having watched me endure a lot of illness, that it was just one of those things. He said, "Have a drink, you'll feel better." The panacea for all problems was always "a drink." I didn't want to appear dramatic, but I insisted that I wanted to go home. Frank suggested that the driver take me, and then return to pick Frank up later. When I got home the *ayah* called the doctor, who immediately came to the house. He suspected that I was having a heart attack.

The doctor went to his office and returned with equipment for an electrocardiograph. The results showed that I was experiencing a "schemic" change in the regularity of the heart, so the doctor ordered bed rest. He said that my pulse rate was a very low 52. He arranged for medication to be delivered, and said that a shot of brandy three times a day would help to increase my heart rate. I knew of no source for brandy, but thought that under these circumstances, someone might be able to procure some for me.

I was so tired that I slept for hours. When Frank came home, he did not want to believe that I had had a heart attack. He patted my hand and kissed my forehead, as though I were a child. I was the main source of his strength, his cheerleader, and it was entirely unacceptable that I had a faulty heart. That was too frightening for him. (His mother had been in a constant state of heart episodes.) Even though I was too weak to get out of bed, Frank did not show concern. The buzz about my episode had zipped through Delhi, and people were calling. A Spanish woman from my club brought me a bottle of brandy. A full month later, the doctor said I would have to leave the country to escape the worst of the heat. I wanted to go.

I was afraid.

During the month following my diagnosis, Frank was cheerful, humoring me as though I were not really ill at all, in spite of the fact that the doctor repeated the electrocardiogram every few days. One evening, when Frank had brought a business friend for dinner, he came into the bedroom and said to me, "Matt is here. Why don't you put on a robe and come in for a drink?" He knew that Matt was one of my favorite people in the company, but he didn't realize how weak I was. I knew that this attitude resulted directly from his experience with the hypochondria in his family when he was a child. And I felt guilty, almost convincing myself that I was just playing a part. Was I trying to persuade my mother that I shouldn't go to school? That's how I felt. Frank told me to "put on my Viking hat" and march into the living room and beat the world. Putting on my Viking hat was an affectionate term he always used when he was referring to any kind of problem that I could solve when nobody else could. He admired my strength. Losing my strength was tantamount to Frank losing his.

How I longed to be looked after. My dear *ayah* sat outside my door, and even slept there. But it was Frank's attention I wanted. At times, I even convinced myself that I was a sham and the heart attack was a figment of my imagination. Even today, when I feel that I'm coming down with the flu or a cold, I make myself get up, make the bed, and dress. Then I allow myself to lie on top of the bed, covered with an afghan. No school tomorrow.

I left India that summer as directed by my doctor. I left with mixed emotions. I felt like the rat leaving the sinking ship. Leaving the children was especially difficult, as it was summer vacation time for them, and there was little for them to do to occupy themselves. A large percentage of children had gone back to their homes in other countries for two months, so it was a socially barren wasteland for that time. The luxury of having a car and driver at their disposal was moot when there were so few friends to visit.

Although Kristin had been horseback riding in the very early hours of the morning, it had become too hot to do that now. Almost all the other women and children had left, so New Delhi was a city filled with abandoned men. I knew that Frank would entertain, as gregarious as he was, and that having kitchen staff would make it easy. I became extremely depressed and self-absorbed, having done nothing in the past month but think. I felt guilty because I was looking forward to visiting dear friends, and my first stop would be in Madrid. I knew how much Frank missed Spain, but he was generous and only wanted what was good for me.

When I saw my best friend at the Madrid airport, I felt like I had come home. It was morning and when we arrived at her house we sat and had coffee, there was so much to talk about. When she took me upstairs to show me an antique chest in their bedroom, she asked me, with a smile, why I was carrying my purse from room to room. I was flustered. "Do you think someone is going to rob you?" she asked. "Yes," I replied. I forgot I was in a different society and surrounded by good Catholic maids.

"You're in great luck, arriving today," my friend said, "There's a big party tonight and I think all the people are friends of yours." I was overjoyed. That evening was an occasion. I was embraced over and over again, and there was real beef for dinner. But my emotions bewildered me. I didn't seem to belong there any more. I had known these people for years, but was surprised to find myself feeling aloof. Or was it they who were aloof? It wasn't until much later that I realized that, odd as it might seem, I had more in common with our friends in India now than I did at that party. In Delhi, we all had something in common, and that was the extreme difficulty of almost everyday living.

I was still easily tired and I found myself sitting in a corner, totally confused. My emotions ran rampant. Where did I belong?

The Good Life

After Spain, I went to Canada. I was greeted by another good friend we had known in Spain and who was now living there. She told me that adjusting to another way of life had been difficult, and that she thought Canadians were not friendly. Our nomadic way of life did bring trauma, however slight, but I was just passing through. Their home was on a beautiful street, and the breeze was fragrant.

On my first visit to a supermarket, I was overwhelmed with the multiple choices and had no idea what to buy. There were products on the shelves I had never heard of. Everything was so bright, so clean, so dazzling. I felt as though I had been in India forever. I was like a complete stranger in my own country.

Going to a department store, I was even more stunned, although I had been dreaming of this for a long time. I actually found myself having a paralyzing anxiety attack. My friend, who understood this experience, put her arm around me and suggested we leave. I had been standing at a counter where women's blouses were displayed. The abundance. The meticulous fabrics. Most of all, I was dizzied by the perfume and cosmetic counters, with all the sweet, glorious scents and beautiful packages.

I had become so accustomed to accepting the least terrible that the offering of just *everything* was more than I could emotionally handle. When I got into the car, I started to cry, and my friend embraced me and didn't have to ask why. I was keenly aware of how much Canadians or Americans take for granted. I truly knew how to count the blessings, which I still do, every day.

Home Again

Letters from Frank were waiting for me at my sister's house in Canada. They were love letters of such sweetness and purity that I read them over and over for many years. He also said the children were going to summer school, which was actually the American school, but they were solely absorbed in arts and crafts, and were, of course, making pottery for me. He said that the staff was taking good care of the children, and when Frank had to travel, they were always safe. But they were also lonely, and they missed me.

Kristin was reading all the Edith Blyton books again, finding comfort in Spanish. My guilt rose in my throat, even though I knew I would not be entertaining the children if I were there, but at least I would simply be there. I felt no regret that the children had not yet completely mastered English phrases when I read Kristin's letter to me, which said, "I am filled with missingness." Could there be a more beautiful word?

Before a month had passed, I was longing to go home to my family. That was where my heart was. I was entertained by my friends and family, and had stopped coveting things and places and homes and cars and all the good material things we had dreamed about. I wanted to go home and be with Frank and John and Kristin and Johanna. I wanted to wake in the morning to hear Frank say, "Hey, it's another sunny day in Delhi!" I knew that my contentment lay with my family, wherever we would be.

The trip back to India was very long and tiring, and of course the plane arrived in the wee hours of the morning, black as pitch. When I came out the front door of the miserable airport, six of our friends, festooned with garlands, were there to serenade me. The garlands were the only things that smelled good, but I was now a veteran.

.

The Cobra Situation

One afternoon, the gate guard came to the door and said there was a snake charmer there who swore that we had a cobra in our garden. Frank and I immediately grasped that yes, we probably did, and wondered who threw it into the garden? He was carrying a sack filled with cobras that he had "taken from our neighbors' gardens." Well, really. Should we call his bluff and send him away? We thought not. He said he would remove all his clothes and leave his sack outside to prove his honesty.

I sat in our parked car but closed my eyes, not because I was afraid of the snake, but because I was less than enchanted with the idea of seeing the snake charmer naked. We paid him ten rupees up front. He played his flute and wandered in the garden, until suddenly a cobra uncoiled itself from beneath a large tree were our children played. He picked up the snake and milked it of its venom, then threw it in his sack. Then he said, "All cobras have mates. You must have another in the garden." Did we want to take a chance? Another deal was made and transacted. The children really enjoyed the show.

"That guy has a good thing going," Frank said. "I kind of admire him."

Animals for Entertainment

Birthdays for children, everyone said, are magical in India. When Johanna's birthday came, we hired a dancing bear, a snake charmer, a performing monkey, and a camel trainer who took the children for rides around the neighborhood.

As I watched the various acts, I found myself feeling more than uncomfortable. The men who brought these animals and who were the performers, so to speak, treated the animals terribly. The bear was mangy and cowering, and the performing monkey was obviously terrified of his master with the pointed stick. I didn't go near enough to the camel on the street, the main reason being that camel breath is an experience one does not want to be exposed to twice.

I looked over at Johanna and she was grimacing, looking away, a tear running down her cheek. After the party, she came to me and said, "Please don't ever ask for animals again. Those men hurt them, and I don't want to watch."

One weekend, we went on an expedition at a wildlife park where we all rode elephants. We were there with Indian friends who had invited us to go and possibly see the tigers in their own habitat. We waited for the tigers from a very high viewing stand, but none appeared. On the way home, in the car, we played I Spy. When it was my turn, I chose the dashboard of the car, and said that I spied something that started with the letter D. The children began guessing, as they looked out the window:

"Dung?"

"Dead person?"

"Dirt?"

"Dead animal?"

What a nice place to live.

The Sacred Cow and the Rescued Pony

Although our house was in a neighborhood that was considered to be very posh, we had to drive through a desperately poor area to get home from the stores. I knew that I had to inure myself to the terrible displays of poverty, or I would not be able to contend with everyday life. Then one day, when we had stopped at a corner, I saw two Sikhs who were playing soccer on the street, using a baby pig for a ball. I rolled down the window and shouted at them to stop. Once again, the driver, always smiling, cautioned me not to interfere, because if I did, he would have to get out of the car to defend me. I hated to ignore this atrocity, but I had learned to listen to the driver.

It was impossible to understand that in a country where the cow is sacred, other animals could be so mistreated. Oxen were used to pull wagons, and they were constantly whipped and prodded anally with long sticks. Yet Hindus do not harm flies, because of their belief that all living things return to the earth after death, in some living form, and that everything living in the present could be a manifestation of a person who has died. This could not be clarified when it applied to the cruelty I had witnessed.

A few weeks before Kristin's birthday, she came to me after school and asked me if I could do something "now" for her birthday. From the school bus, she had seen a small horse that was scarred and beaten, which she had witnessed, and she begged me to get the driver and go with her to find the horse and buy it. She said she had to save it. I admired her for her empathy, but I doubted we would find the horse. Kristin insisted the horse could be kept at the back of our garden, near a tree, and she would look after it.

I agreed to call the driver and look for the horse. She directed us to the street and as we slowly drove, she saw it: it was a small pony. I asked Sharma to park the car and walk to where the pony was standing, as though the transaction were on his part, but the owner had already seen our car, and demanded a high price, too much for the value of the pony, but acceptable for Kristin's act of kindness. We bought the pony and tied her loosely to a tree in the back yard. Sharma bought a feedbag and oats. Kristin visited the horse every day, brushing its torn coat. It was a sedentary life, but at least it was a life without abuse.

The Mayonnaise Adventure

In the early weeks of living in the house, I had fired the cook and the bearer for stealing. In the interim I had flared my nostrils and pranced into the kitchen to make mayonnaise. The kitchen was so unbelievably hot, my clothes were sticking to my back and my hair was plastered to my head. I took off my cotton blouse and pants, and was trying to mix oil and eggs and vinegar in a bowl, with little success, but this was a crisis. We had bread and cooked chicken to make sandwiches for the children's lunch, and mayonnaise was a must.

I heard someone come in the front door, and when I looked up, I saw an Indian friend who knew the guards at the gate and had been waved in. Without exception, he was our closest Indian friend, and the guards knew that. I began a tirade about how the hell was mayonnaise made and he looked down at the recipe and said it looked like the right ingredients, but the consistency of my bowl full of glop was obviously not thick enough to be mayonnaise. This, by the way, was during a power failure, so I couldn't use the blender.

"Let's try whipping it with a wooden spoon," he said. Yes, sir. I handed him an egg and turned the project over to him. "Let's put another yolk in," he said, "before the eggs go bad." "We'd better get this done right now," he said. Side by side, we addressed the project, whipping and beating, but the result was a disaster.

"We have a jar of American mayonnaise at home," he said. "I'll just drive home and put some in a jar for you." I said that would be great. When he left, I started cleaning up the counters, and realized that not for a minute had either one of us mentioned the fact that I was in my panties and bra.

Sights and Sounds at 4:00 a.m.

All international flights out of Delhi left after midnight, in the wee hours of the morning, and 4:00 a.m. seemed to be the most common hour, so those who were leaving were treated to a carnival of orifices blowing in the wind. It is the religious custom that all orifices of the body must be cleansed and purged early in the day, which is probably a fine contribution to the smells of India. When one considers the openings about which we speak, it can well be imagined that this is not a pretty sight. Noses honk, mouths spit, bladders are flushed, and bowels are blown and emptied. Cold water is snuffed up the nose and into the mouth and throat. None of this pageant is conducted behind closed doors, for indeed the preponderance of these people had no doors, and the great open spaces belonged to them . . . fields, front yards, ditches, preferably in plain view of cars on the main road. Bare bottoms are displayed with abandon. As can be imagined, there is a certain amount of sound that accompanies this ceremony, and the hawks and spits and the booms and the snorting are blessedly not audible from a moving car. But when these people live close to your house, these sounds are as common as the crowing of a rooster.

The School: AIS becomes AES

The American International School in New Delhi was an excellent school. I remember the fifth grade teacher, a young man of less than thirty years, who had made a sign that hung over the door to his classroom and that said: "Through these portals pass the most important people in my world."

The school was called the American International School (AIS) but soon after we arrived, Indira Gandhi proclaimed that the school name must be changed to the American Embassy School (AES). The purpose of this was to deny Indian children enrollment at the school, which meant that those who had already been attending were now forced to leave. Mrs. Gandhi was vehemently anti-American.

An American friend of mine who was married to an Indian had to face a fierce battle trying to keep her two sons in the school. At the time, they were in junior high school, preparatory to qualifying for entrance to an American university. They'd been attending the school since they were in elementary. As her sons had dual citizenship and carried American passports, they were reluctantly allowed to stay. All other Indian students were forced to leave.

It was because of this caveat that only embassy children could have lunch in the cafeteria.

The one time I saw Indira Gandhi in person was at an Indian wedding. I was stunned that she was such a petite woman, not much more than five feet tall, but her intense presence was palpable. A pathway was cleared for her to approach the bridal couple. When a small plate was offered to her, her bodyguard tasted the food before she took a bite. The plate held only peanuts, which we learned was a rule when Mrs. Gandhi was in attendance. After this small ritual, she departed. I swore to Frank that she gave me a nasty look, as we were the only non-Indian faces there.

Making Friends with a Local

Frank had quite a number of Indian acquaintances connected with his work. They were factory owners and traders who were very wealthy and well educated. One of these men came to visit on his way home from a trip through Europe. He was a carpet factory owner, and had been in our home on several occasions for dinner or drinks. On that particular night, he became very drunk, and when he was preparing to leave, I noticed that he was staggering a bit. He was carrying a coat, which he had needed for his trip through cold countries, and as he put it over his arm, he almost lost his balance.

I suggested to him that he spend the night in our guest room, rather than leave in his condition. He demurred, but I took his coat from him, and when I did, a bottle of scotch fell on the floor from inside his coat. He had stolen it from the bar (bootleg whisky is recognizable). Why? This man could afford to buy a distillery and most certainly could bribe all the customs officers in India if he wanted to import liquor.

When I went into the bedroom to turn down the bed, he lurched after me and tried to kiss me and wrestle me onto the bed. I was disgusted and easily escaped his advances. I knew this wouldn't have happened if he hadn't been drinking. When I went to our bedroom, I told Frank about the entire unpleasant episode, and without looking up from his book, he said, "It pisses me off about the scotch." In difficult times, our values change.

Merry Feces to You

During the Christmas season, when Frank and I were driving downtown to try to find some presents for the children, we drove with the windows open, and just as we were driving through a rather shabby residential district, we were suddenly pelted with what we thought were dirty stones, but soon realized were human feces. And all the best of the holiday season to you too, merry gentlemen.

That evening, at a dinner party, I was seated beside a wry foreign correspondent, one of my favorite dinner companions, and I told him what had happened. "Well," he said, "it beats the hell out of indifference."

The Black Market

Every now and then black market foods were sold in certain shops, set at whatever price they chose. We were willing to pay. One evening, we got a call from an Indian friend, saying he had found a small jar of Kraft cheese, and would we like to come over and have a drink with crackers and cheese.

When we arrived, we saw the small jar, the size of a juice jar, in the middle of the coffee table. We took turns eating crackers and glancing at each other to make sure we didn't take too much. It was like a religious rite. And it was pimento, a cheese I didn't even like. But oh, how we missed cheese!

The sense of sharing amongst those of us who lived on the local economy was a constant. On another occasion, a German friend called to say he had a can of Maxwell House coffee and invited us for lunch, after which we actually watched the coffee percolating. Conversation was hushed. This was a holy moment. Coffee was available from the regular market, but the local coffee tasted different.

Occasionally, I found jars of jam or cocktail sausage (which would be too plebeian to serve in the U.S., but was exotic now) and once, peanut butter, the most coveted food of all for those who had children. I asked the proprietor where it all came from, and he said that diplomats from the Middle East who didn't drink alcohol made a profit bootlegging it to distributors. We were glad they did.

Silk and Bread

How could anyone with ten servants say she had a hard life? True, I didn't clean or cook, and the laundry was done and fresh flowers were in place every day. It was the life of the raj, I suppose. I would have traded that life in a heartbeat to live in a small house in a civilized country, and I wouldn't have ever minded preparing the meals or doing the laundry. I definitely would not mind shopping for groceries.

Throughout our stay in India, people from Frank's cover company came on business trips and sometimes brought their wives. One wife told me how much she loved India, with all its antiques and brass and silk. It was a fantastic shopping spree. And, of course, meals were taken either in the hotel or with us at our home. One of the wives I particularly liked, and I went shopping with her. Without any exposure to the hardship of everyday living, I could actually see her point. They always travelled to India in the winter months when the heat was not hellish. They had our car and driver at their disposal, and our home was welcoming and teeming with servants in white coats.

I search my memory for Hallmark moments. Those that

come to mind were the times when we shared what we had, in a place where even the smallest luxury was an occasion, and I mean a jar of strawberry jam, not four yards of silk. It was a question of values.

One of the best birthday presents I ever had was given to me in India. A woman whom I knew slightly, and who, for some reason, knew when my birthday was, dropped in with a gift-wrapped package. When I untied the ribbon and unwrapped the package, there was a loaf of Wonder Bread (she had embassy commissary privileges.) I nearly cried. There had been no flour on the local market for weeks.

The Transfer

From the very first day we arrived in India, Frank had kept a large calendar on the wall, and now the last days were being ticked off, with large black Xs. We were looking forward to moving. Frank went to Washington for his annual trip, and while there he miraculously reached me by phone, and said that he was asked to go to Japan as our next post.

I was stunned. It made government sense that the fact that we all spoke fluent Spanish would qualify us perfectly for Japan. I was not elated. At this point, I was already dreaming of home, although I didn't know where home was. I had no particular dream about a house with a white picket fence, and certainly did not have a vision of Frank barbecuing in the backyard. But. Something like that. Frank kept telling me that what I was dreaming about just didn't exist, and that now that our lives had so richly been interrupted, I would be a different person.

When Frank came back from Washington, we had a long talk about what we would do. He said that he felt sure the move to

Japan would bring about the promotion that had been withheld from him, particularly because we would first spend a year at an Ivy League campus, famous for its linguistic department, where he would study Japanese with total immersion. We both knew that would be hard for him. Frank knew that I had been unhappy in India, and so had he. He said he would not accept the new post if that was what I chose.

I thought about our situation for a long time, and facing reality, saw that if Frank were to stay with the Agency, there appeared to be no alternative dream assignment. His option would be to take a desk job in Washington. We had no money to invest in a house, and the children would go to public schools, but more than anything else, I very seriously considered what our life would be like if Frank was forced to work in a cubicle in Langley. He would be in hell. This man who loved the work as he did, and knew that it had value, work that gave him a sense of accomplishment and pride, could not be imprisoned in an office. The entire family would be unhappy. Even from a selfish point of view, I knew that Frank should accept the new post in Japan. It would be best for all of us. International schools were excellent, and the tuition was paid. We could not return to America and live on a salary lower than that of a garbage collector. Not when we had been living the life of a raj.

I had never met a Japanese person, but had seen them alighting from tour buses and entering hotels, where they all stood obediently, waiting for the tour guide's instructions. When I noticed a group in our hotel in New Delhi, I was struck by the fact that even their luggage was all the same, as though they had purchased it as an adjunct to the cost of the tour. How did they know which luggage was theirs, I wondered. Movies had depicted the language as being menacing and growling.

Common sense dictated that my impression was superficial

and probably did not represent the Japanese in their own country, going about the activities of their daily lives. This was the only location offered to us, and we would stay with the same cover company, so that was a huge bonus.

We agreed to go to Japan.

Our Departure

We had made good friends of every nationality and background during our stay in India, and when we left, joyous parties were held for us, acknowledging the abundance of sharing and friendship, the depth of which could only have been found in a third world country, or as Frank described it, "the night soil circuit." (Night soil is human excrement collected from buckets, cesspools and outhouses and sometimes used as manure.)

And we did leave on July 17th at 4:00 a.m. on Lufthansa, destined for Frankfurt. The general manager of Lufthansa was a friend of ours and he partied with us the night we left. He sent an Indian employee with us to make sure that our departure was smooth. After Frank went through the scanner, which was not a machine but an Indian inspector, the Lufthansa employee who had escorted us started to run after Frank, who was galloping toward the airplane. The man followed in rapid pursuit, waving something in his hand, shouting, "Sir! Sir! He took your wallet!" Frank kept running toward the plane, which was on the tarmac, and shouted back, "Keep it! Keep it! It's poetic!" But he did get his wallet back and we got on the plane and smiled. And smiled and smiled and smiled.

As I try to dredge up good memories of the time spent in India, I have great difficulty coming up with one whole good day. Influenced as I was by the fact that my health had failed from the first day I arrived, I make an effort to remove myself from that, and to consider the whole picture. There were definitely happy times when we had been to parties with our circle of friends, and times when we entertained at home. We became well acquainted with the buyers from the cover company and, in retrospect, we got to know them all personally. They always spent time in our home, because almost all of them had been sick during previous visits and welcomed a respite. One buyer had refused to visit India again, until he knew he could stay with us in our home. And all of this augured well for Frank and his fine reputation with the cover company. The branch of the company had more than prospered under his direction.

I had redecorated the house and everyone commented on its beauty. Where else could I have curtain fabric woven to my specific request . . . sheer silk with gold thread running through it? And rosewood tables and carved chairs, beautifully crafted and polished by hand? These things followed us everywhere when we moved.

I wasn't afraid of the people, but the circumstances under which we lived were frightening, because I did not understand the culture or the language. The one trip to Old Delhi had absolutely terrified me and was indelible in my memory. It was visceral and influenced me always.

Later in our lives, when we were reunited with friends we had made in India, the reunions were especially sweet. At one of our farewell parties before departing India, a dear Indian friend said to Frank, "Will we ever see you again?" And Frank said, "Of course. We may be living someplace else, but we will always summer in India." There was always the laughter. It was a life lesson.

I feel slightly less guilty about my judgment of life in India when I think of the three non-Indian women who had married Indians. Two were American and one was British. When

I talked to them about my unhappiness there, the unanimous reaction was "Look at us! We're condemned to stay here!" Condemned was the word they used.

We did have strong bonds with the other foreigners who were there when we were. In most places, it is said that we talk about the weather because it's the one thing we have in common. In New Delhi we talked about our intestinal tracts.

I think India was a good experience for the children because they were not exposed to the difficulties that confronted me. Kristin took riding lessons, at 5:00 a.m. to escape the heat, and was driven to the stables by our driver. She became a passionate horsewoman and rode in dressage horse shows at the famous Red Fort. John played soccer with the British school. And Johanna became friends with Sharma's 14-year old daughter, Madhu. They were six years apart and didn't speak each other's languages but they spent every afternoon together after school, riding their bicycles or sneaking off to the servant's quarters to help Madhu's mother make dinner. All three children made fast friends while there, and not too long ago Kristin found a childhood friend from that period. When she called, it was as though no time had passed. They talked about how much fun India was. I'm glad.

We had a few Indian friends who were for the most part educated abroad and this made a difference. They had seen Paree. And they could stand back and look at their own country objectively, not with bitterness, but with amusement.

Everyone we knew counted the days until he could leave. Perhaps the people who lived under the protective umbrella of the embassy had an easier life, but we didn't know them.

The Year of the Ivy League (1974-1975)

Contentment

We sublet a clapboard house on stilts, with floor-to-ceiling windows filtering the autumn sunlight. It was at the end of a long and winding driveway, set in a glade in the middle of the woods with a path to an enormous pond for swimming or ice skating. There were deer grazing calmly from the edge of the yard, and apple trees and tomato plants and a deck, which wandered all the way around the house. There was a television and stereo and a washing machine and dryer. There were ice cubes from the refrigerator and water from the faucet and milk from a cow, and a huge supermarket. There was clean, clean air and the glory of the changing leaves and the smell of smoke from the chimneys and a phone that worked. There were price tags on everything and Carly Simon on the car radio, and bakeries and wine shops with every kind of cheese. There was feeling safe all the time and stopping the car to look down at the placid lake, and movies to watch and neighbors to chat with. There were wool scarves and boots and Thanksgiving with old friends watching the football game, and John Denver singing, "Gee, it's great to be back home again." There were floating snowflakes on Christmas Day and a huge, sparkling Christmas tree and a monstrous fireplace. Every morning I was glad. We had everything.

I hadn't known that campus buildings in the Ivy League were truly covered with ivy. Everything smelled good. An orange school bus stopped at the end of the driveway to take the children to school, and nobody wanted to kill them.

My ugly green station wagon cost six hundred dollars, and we could pile skis and bicycles and children in the back, and slide into a ditch in a blizzard knowing that the man in the house nearby will call a tow truck and offer me coffee. I was content.

Me the Driver

This was a hard time for Frank, because his Japanese class was an intensive crash course, three years in one, shared by young graduate students who had studied the language before. Other businessmen had tried, but none had stayed, in most cases because they fell so far behind. It was a small class, self-propelled, and the pressure was intense. Frank was determined to get through it with a passing grade. He got up at 5:00 a.m. after sleeping just a few hours, and plugged in to his Walkman, pacing, muttering Japanese phrases and very tired.

After experiencing severe tooth pain, Frank visited a local dentist who told him that he needed oral surgery. He recommended an oral surgeon in a city a hundred miles away. Because he would be heavily sedated, he was told he couldn't drive, making it obvious that I would have to drive him. I had just obtained my driver's license two weeks earlier, and dreaded this drive in my terrible car. Frank drove on the way up, and the surgery took two hours, after which he was like a sleepwalker, leaning heavily on me to get to the car. It had begun to snow. I had never driven in snow, but sure, I could do this. Frank fell into a stupor in the car, his head lolling down his chest. I turned on the windshield wipers, and discovered they couldn't handle snow.

The rest of the drive was terrifying. I could not see where I was going, so I jumped in and out of the car, wiping the snow away from the windshield. Frank slept on. I could not read the signs. Had I driven into another state? Oh my God. Please, God, I said quietly, guide me home. Other cars were turning onto what looked like a highway that we had driven on that morning. I took a chance, muttering my pleas to God and the Virgin Mary and anyone else who might listen. I was on the right highway. I drove slowly from there, until finally I saw the mailbox at the end of our driveway. Thank you, God and the Virgin.

All I could think of was a hot cup of tea. I put the kettle on, rubbing my nearly frozen hands together. I put a teacup beside the stove, and hugging myself, I looked out the kitchen window at the blizzard. Then I realized that I had left Frank in the car. I scrambled down the steps to the car. Frank was still apparently unconscious. I shook him and said we were home, and helped him up the stairs. I never admitted to him that I had forgotten him in the car. "The wipers don't work very well," I told him later.

When the anesthetic wore off, Frank was in excruciating pain. His mouth had numerous stitches and was packed with gauze. The painkiller didn't help much. He insisted the next day that he could not miss class. His face was swollen and ashen. He was trying to drink warm orange juice through a straw when he slid off his chair in a dead faint. I called the professor and said my boy Frank would not be in school today. I knew he would rather I had schlepped his unconscious body into the station wagon and driven to school. I guess he thought he could trust me.

Frank was the mascot of the class, an old-timer at forty, always charming and funny, with self-deprecating humor that endeared him to his classmates. When a young woman in Frank's class, in the bloom of idealism and spirituality, asked him, "What did your experience in India teach you? What did you learn from that incredible country?" He replied, "Always drive six car lengths behind an elephant."

There seemed to be no generation gap in his relationship with the other students, and they always hung around our house for swimming and meals and beer drinking. They rooted for him all the way and applauded when he passed, tutored him when he flagged. He made it through the entire term with a passing grade.

He was the celebrity of his class.

He said it was the hardest thing he had ever done in his life.

Back to School

At the beginning of the school term, we were advised that I, too, could attend classes at the university where Frank was learning Japanese. That mandate was not specific, and I was eager to take advantage of their excellent drama department to study playwriting, an opportunity that wouldn't repeat itself in my future. I knew I could study Japanese in Japan.

I was not the mascot of my class of eighteen-year-olds because I didn't have the fashion sense demanded. Instead of wearing oversized overalls and army boots, I dared to attend class in a black pants suit. I was, however, teacher's pet, because I was the only one who paid attention, took notes, and did my homework. When we were assigned to write a one-act play, we were asked, at random, to read the play aloud. After listening to two students read their work, I realized I would be considered mundane, even boring, as I had not once used "fuck you" or "motherfucker" or "shit" in every other utterance. My drawing-room setting and sophisticated banter elicited raised eyebrows and a rolling of the eyes. When I was leaving class and walking toward my car, one of the other students was walking with me, and a passing professor nodded toward me and said hello. "I don't know him," I said. "Yeah, well, he knows me," the young man responded, "and he probably thinks you're my mother." How sharper than a serpent's tooth.

The children once again had to face the cliques of the public schools, Johanna at an elementary school, John and Kristin at a junior high. Early on, they learned not to talk about their foreign experience, because the reaction was usually that of someone who had just met a space alien. They quickly excelled in their classes, discovering that international schools are far more demanding. In a short time, they became bored and even lost interest in television, drifting back to their books. John took a renewed interest in the guitar, now learning to play rock and roll. "When are we going to Japan?" Kristin asked one day. "The kids here are all blond and boring."

They already knew that the world was a place of variables, that life had different flavors and colors and languages. It was the seeding of sophistication. I think I was pleased, but I wasn't sure. At least we knew there would be no emotional wrench when we left. The wrench would be all mine. I was enjoying my life, but I also felt that I couldn't demonstrate this too vividly, because I was a Good Wife and Good Mother.

It became clear that I really didn't belong in that area when I attended a mother/teacher meeting at Johanna's school. The school was located in a bucolic setting and most of the students were children of farmers. Once more, I did not know the dress code and that the accepted garb was a quilted parka and boots, and even rollers in the hair. It was the pants suit gaffe again. I just couldn't wear that anywhere.

I slipped up on proper protocol another time, when I called a repairman to fix the furnace. He was a young, breezy, personable young man. When he went down the basement stairs, I followed him and stood there while he was looking for the trouble. The basement was dark and cold. After a while, I realized he was looking at me strangely. Was I demonstrating the "bored wife syndrome"? It was the influence of India where any workman had to be carefully watched so he wouldn't steal. How could I explain this to him? I fled up the stairs.

I recognized the way in which our children were different from their classmates when Kristin, who had just received a letter from a friend saying that her family was being posted in Korea, asked, "Couldn't I fly to Korea from Japan to visit her?" My initial reaction was that the suggestion was ridiculous, she was only twelve years old. But Frank replied, "Sure, why not?" And later, she did go to Korea by herself. She was fine. The passport and customs situation was old hat.

During the respite in America, I felt comfortable with the lifestyle. I never felt nostalgia for a life with servants; that had never been the good life to me. The most profound glitch was that during the entire time we were there, Frank was under such extreme pressure that he barely communicated with me at all. He was totally consumed with his goal to succeed. Even during the Easter break when he was free for three weeks to relax by the pond or enjoy any other pastime, he remained quiet and distant. He had always been competitive, always at the top of his class, and that could never change. He showed a polite interest in the classes I was taking, but never asked to read any of my writing. He didn't have the time. I felt rejected during the entire time he was at the university, even though I understood the demands he put upon himself.

We had not been in a position to make friends, and it had been convenient and fun that his classmates enjoyed coming to our house, because they were free when Frank was free, and I delighted in their company. One Sunday when the gang was all there, Frank and I were talking about going out for drinks and dinner on my birthday. His pretty young tutor said, "Why don't you take her to that place where you took me to lunch?" I felt hurt by that. I had noticed that she was flirtatious with Frank, almost wanting me to notice, tossing her hair and glancing at me. I decided to ignore it.

What was apparent to me was that it would be impossible for us to live in a prosaic atmosphere in the United States when all of Frank's dreams revolved around living a much more exciting life. We were at odds about what made us happy and fulfilled. I was saddened by the fact that this was the turn our life had taken. Had I promised this in our wedding vows? I married an airline pilot. I had spent hours with a Catholic priest, not to become a Catholic but to be clear about what was expected when I married a Catholic. I had conceded enough.

I was either going to have to martyr myself in the true sense, and move on with the family, or take a stand and resign. There was no question that there was no question. The rock and the hard place. I was never unsure of Frank's love and high regard for me. If I had sincerely asked him to reject the move to Japan for my sake, I knew he would listen and would be sympathetic. If he had to take a desk job in Washington, I would feel like I had broken his spirit and he'd be miserable. I wanted his happiness for my own sake. When Frank was happy, he exuded joy, and I would be a part of that. My choice was obvious. And ultimately, I guess it was for myself.

During our stay at the university, Frank received a call from our Indian friend, Ashok. He was settling into his new post in Washington, and said he was "radiant." He wanted to thank Frank for standing by him. Frank was very pleased for Ashok. Frank had won the battle, but he had lost the war. It was a high price to pay.

Shopping for a Move Abroad

Before leaving for Japan, I wrote to one of the executive's wives in Tokyo, to inquire about conditions there. I had been told that she had four children, and I asked about whether I should be getting a year's supply of clothes for my children, as I had to do in other countries. The purchases I had made prior to our move to India turned out to be ludicrous (such as leather shoes in graduated sizes, when only sandals were ever worn).

Her reply suggested that I buy as much of the children's wardrobe as possible. That it would be wise to buy jeans and shirts and shoes. She also suggested that I be careful about the length of the then-popular bell-bottom jeans, because the streets of Tokyo were very dirty. After the country I had just left, I really wasn't too concerned about any health hazard that the streets of Japan might threaten. I hated the annual purchase of clothing, not just for the kids, but all of us. There was always a quandary about the clothes Frank and I needed, without having a hint of what our lifestyle would be like there. Our budget was very limited and I wasn't able to splurge. I had always thought the Agency should have given us a clothing allowance when it was necessary for us to revise entire wardrobes to lend to the style and weight required by the weather or the seasons.

I had to settle for two cocktail type dresses for me. During our stay in India, I had been able to collect long skirts and silk pants from the sari silks that were available. Tailoring had been cheap there, and Frank had an attractive wardrobe, which included suits. The shopping for the children was hell. They were now at the age when they wanted to make their own selections, so when I took them to a department store, they all went off in different directions, choosing entirely inappropriate styles for their age or the predicted weather. Any mother of teenagers will understand the frustration of shopping with them for just one pair of pants. It was a battle. I used to get so distressed and impatient, that I told them I was posting myself at a mezzanine coffee shop, and after they had collected their stash, I could be summoned for approval and payment. Once, I actually cried. I sat with my coffee and wept because I felt like leaving the store in the hope that a stranger might kidnap them and the whole problem would be solved.

We managed to get through that shopping day without personal injury, staggering under the shopping bags filled with clothes, which inevitably either didn't fit or were unsuitable. John, to his delight, grew nine inches that year, ending his apprehension that he would never be tall. We threw out the clothes for a shorter guy. And we didn't worry about the streets of Tokyo being dirty, because in fact they weren't. I saw not one cow patty anywhere near our house.

I think back to the insane shopping that I did in Madrid before moving to New Delhi. This included those leather shoes in staggered sizes, all of which were never worn in that climate. I had also shopped for a washing machine and dryer in Madrid, having found that Frank could not purchase these in the U.S. It turned out that the entire purchase was useless because of the frequent power outages. Everyone in India had a *dhobi* who pounded the dirt out of the clothes with a rock in the bathtub. My quest for a refrigerator was complicated because

I was insistent that it include an ice-maker, party-givers that we were. I wasn't sufficiently knowledgeable to realize that we could not use ice cubes from the water pipes. I had forgotten to buy ice trays to use with boiled water, one of those small oversights needed to further complicate the move, just enough to tear out my hair.

As I had been assured that Tokyo was probably the most uptown city anyone could live in, and that everything was available at a price, I did not concern myself with packing foodstuffs. I wished I had stashed a case of pantyhose, though. I had thought that because I am not tall, I could wear what Japanese women wear. It turned out that I had to become accustomed to a crab-like form of walking, because the crotch of my Japanese hose was halfway to my knees.

This is really incidental stuff, but it becomes horrendously important when this seems to be your constant business. Moving, buying, packing. It was very hard, no matter where we were going, and I was always astonished at how wrong the information was when I asked for it. Particularly when the U.S. Embassy grandly offered to send me a printout from their State Department catalog, or whatever it was called. One fact that enriched my life was that the average temperature in New Delhi, India, was 74 degrees. After that gem of information, I did not ask for their advice again.

An American friend in New Delhi had lived in the night soil circuit for many years. She was sanguine about that invasive and cavalier search of luggage each time she came back to India after her trip home. She knew the customs men always stole American candy, so she piled her suitcase with extra large bars of chocolate, which was called Ex-Lax. We could only smile dreamily, imagining the results.

Japan (1975-1981)

The Neighborhood

When we arrived in Tokyo, our first home was the Hilton Hotel. Frank was immediately whisked away on an orientation sweep of East Asia since his territory also covered Korea and Hong Kong. There were four American executives in his office, but only the general manager knew what his true role was. With their help, I found a western-style house with a walled garden, in the heart of an enclave of other such houses. We had a neighborhood! We had a shopping area I could walk to.

When Frank and I accompanied the children to the American School, carrying our written instructions with us, we behaved as though we were undaunted by having to transfer to three different trains, and then going on a mile-long walk to the school. We probably would have been better off sending them by themselves, because we seemed incapable of figuring out which side of the track we were supposed to be on, or how fast we had to run and jump into the train before our arms were severed by the doors. As a result, we found that the third train we were on was the wrong one. The loud announcements of the train stations were unintelligible although the kids could decipher them. I made a promise to myself that I would never have occasion to make this trip alone because God knows where I would have ended up. I felt great dismay, thinking that our

children would have to go through this drill twice a day . . .
just finding their way to school? Let alone, figuring out how
to go anywhere else in Tokyo.

It was such a joy to have friends around the corner to help
me through the "where" and the "how" stage of living in a
foreign country. When we moved in, most of our fellow foreign neighbors were away on their summer vacations, but the
week before school started, they held a cocktail party for all the
newcomers. My immediate impression was that these multi-
nationals were all good friends, and it was a noisy welcome.
We knew we were going to enjoy this group of neighbors.

When school began, groups of neighborhood kids would
meet "under the tree" at the entrance to the neighborhood
compound to start their commute. The train trip became a
social event as more teenagers boarded at each stop. There was
doubt that the Japanese passengers were thrilled with these
boisterous kids. The school day was long, but there was no
complaint about the 6:30 a.m. wake-up call every morning.

I began to study Japanese with a tutor who lived within
walking-distance from our house. To my surprise, I really liked
it, even if I had no expectation of ever using it in conversation. The shops on the street were beautifully kept and it was
not long before shopkeepers greeted me as I walked by. They
always greeted me with the utmost courtesy and smiles, and
they pretended to be thrilled that I could say good morning
and thank you. When the movers came with our furniture, it
seemed like a thousand Japanese men jumped out of the truck,
like the Keystone Cops, quickly propelled themselves all over
the house, putting everything in its proper place, hanging
light fixtures, arranging cushions, putting dishes in the kitchen
cupboards, bowing and smiling and running, and cleaning up
every scrap of paper and every box before they left. It was like

a cheerful invasion. At one point, a man who was hanging a very elaborate brass light fixture, called to me from the top of the ladder. "Denkyu," he said, and I replied, "You're welcome," then he repeated his gracious comment and smiled again. It wasn't until later that I learned that *denkyu* means light bulb in Japanese.

One reason I was glad we were going to be in Japan is that I had never found a cure for my terrible and frequent headaches. I knew the Japanese have numerous acupuncturists and that they are used more frequently than doctors. I asked Frank's secretary if she could find one in my neighborhood and she said it was an easy task. The acupuncturist's office was actually a very small Japanese house on the street where I shopped. I entered, left my shoes in the hall, and took a seat in his very modest treatment room. He entered from another door, and it took a few minutes before I realized that he was blind. His eyes were covered with white film. This was going to be dicey, as I had brought my Japanese dictionary with me, and had planned to point out the painful area in my shoulder and back. I knew the word for wife, and asked him if "there was a wife?" and he said yes, and exited through the same door into his living quarters. Then his wife appeared. White film over the eyes again. Guess this hadn't been love at first sight.

I had no cause to worry. When I lay on my stomach on the table, he pressed his hands on my back and immediately pinpointed the exact place where I had muscle spasms.

Later, when I told this story to a Japanese neighbor, she said that many of the acupuncturists in Japan were blind. They are believed to have a more sensitive and insightful touch. After a few appointments with him, my headaches started to abate for the first time in years.

The Boys in the Back Room

Frank's CIA work in Tokyo was different from the system he had become used to in other countries when he operated alone. He was accustomed to handling every aspect of dealing with agents. He'd arranged the meetings, he did all the dead-drops, he summarized all the reports, and he alone met with the contacts he was responsible for. I had also been frequently involved, because he couldn't spread himself too thin. I have to admit it had been exciting, plotting together, but I was relieved to also just be Frank's wife. He had other people now, probably more savvy than I, but not as sly.

There were four other deep cover men who worked with Frank in Japan, and they were experienced, smart, and capable. All of them had lived in other foreign countries, including the night soil circuit. There is an immediate bond when you meet people who have experienced and understand the hardship post. Frank liked these men personally and admired them professionally. They convened as a group, called "the cluster," and made decisions together, not unlike a board of directors at a company. Socializing with the men in this group was forbidden, but as chance would have it, they had children in the American School who were acquainted with our children and who were involved in the same school activities, especially sports, so this provided a very logical reason for us to become friends, to attend each other's parties or meet for a drink.

We had to be circumspect about all of us being at the same dinner party without other people, but we managed it now and then. The orchestration of one such dinner was very complicated. Much more complicated than necessary, I thought, but then, I thought most of the convoluted schemes they came up with would only indicate guilt. My feeling was that the less underhanded we were, the less people would be suspicious. Like in a secret love affair . . . if the couple meets in public, openly embrace, and sit down to dinner, who is going to notice? Of course, a dinner party with four couples was not in that category.

First, we all took a train to Yokohama, but not the same train. We were not allowed to convene at a train station when we arrived. Instead, we were to walk to a parking lot, where our host would pick us up, one couple at a time. I thought the whole plan was very Maxwell Smart. When we were all assembled, there was a long cocktail "hour." Booze was a crucial commodity for this ensemble. The men spilled with verbosity, the first time being with their own kind, so to speak, and not having to watch their language, nor, from necessity, speak cautiously. It was better than a school reunion. It was more like a gathering of war veterans.

At the dinner table, the men continued to control the conversation, and the women were silent. Perhaps the men should have met by themselves, like members of a twelve-step program. The women were merely appendages. That was difficult. We were the fabric that held these guys together, who lied for them, who spent too many nights alone, who were afraid. This was no different from the business dinners that real people had. I felt tired. I didn't want to be there. I thought it was strange that we didn't even know the name of the host.

We got together with the four men of the cluster and their wives on other occasions. When, after five years, Frank was finally promoted, one of the special agents invited us to dinner at his home to celebrate this long-awaited event. Promotions were a sensitive subject, though. One of the other men had been hoping for a promotion. We all were experiencing financial difficulty all the time, pretending we were rich executives. When the host made a toast to Frank at the dinner table, congratulating him, the wife of his colleague blew up, her anger bringing her to tears. To her, Frank was the new guy. She didn't know that he had been blackballed years before and hadn't received a promotion until now. She left the table weeping. My heart was with her. I had felt that way many times. She was standing up for her husband, and voicing her own indignation. I understood and felt empathy. In a way, it felt strange to feel free to talk about who we were, as though we were airing our dirty laundry, but it was a relief to stop pretending. Over time, this woman and I developed a special bond of friendship.

Frank was still meeting agents in hotels, but now he would spend the night. When he left his cover job for the day, he would carry a gym bag when he left the office, supposedly to go the gym. He was actually carrying a change of clothes. Once when he entered the hotel and was about to register, he saw a neighbor of ours in the lobby, and she saw him. She was there to greet friends who were arriving. They exchanged pleasantries, and Frank casually went into the bar and ordered a drink.

It was quite possible that this chance meeting caused gossip to spread for the wrong reasons, but nevertheless, it would revert to me. My husband had been caught with an overnight bag in the hotel. If necessary, I would be his alibi. Think fast! She never mentioned it, which was significant in itself.

Frank had reached a plateau in his career and this was causing him to become cynical about his work, but not because he didn't like it. He loved what he was doing and he liked his associates. He considered his job to be a noble pursuit, but he found that when he was dealing with an agent who was, of course, a traitor to his country and was apprehensive about being caught, the agent would do almost anything for the right amount of money. A great deal of money.

Frank was proud enough of what he was doing that he turned down enormously attractive offers from other business firms, even though we were barely scraping by from month to month. His passion for his job was an addiction. A little bit of danger with an occasional dash of fear, and you have a happy man.

Nickel and Diming

The ongoing war with the CIA bean counters was a subject of bitter discussions. We felt that the accountants in Washington must think we were living a life of luxury because our rent was paid, especially when the rent was $5,000 a month, which was a normal amount for Tokyo. We didn't even have a car… a business executive without a car? Our neighbors had large sedans and drivers who picked them up in the morning. Still, our expense accounts were scrutinized as though we were all criminals. The discrepancies were picayune. One of Frank's associates had been waiting to meet an agent on a street corner and after standing there for a long time, he decided to have a shoeshine on the street, to cover up his loitering. The bean counters turned down the ten-dollar item, and it became a cause célèbre and a point of pride to fight for. He would not back down, and went so far as to interface with the people in Washington. We cheered.

During their cluster meetings in hotels, the men were not allowed to use room service, or order a meal under any kind of circumstance, regardless of the fact that sometimes the meetings went on for several hours, through either the lunch or dinner hour. When Frank stayed overnight in a hotel, he could not order breakfast from room service. The only items allowed were mixes for drinks and ice, which were ordered before the agent arrived, thereby unseen by the waiter. Frank would actually bring a ginger ale home if it had not been used with drinks. Nobody at home drank ginger ale, but that was not the point.

Etiquette

Although Frank could speak Japanese in only the most honorific form, what was more important was the lesson in protocol. Protocol is everything in this most formal of Asian countries, and the nuances can be baffling. Luckily, the Ivy League university had the good sense to teach the Japanese language students about bowing, presenting business cards, and how to serve tea (the latter being more complicated than the choreography of a ballet).

The man who bows the least is the most important, and the most respected. These were some of the rules: Don't bow at all until you've looked at the other man's business card. This act is deft and slippery. If one business card indicates a sales manager and the other the president of a company, any company, the sales manager must bow deeply and the other man should bow only slightly. This was fondly referred to as the "*meishi* dance," *meishi* meaning the business card. It can be very confusing because the glance at the card is almost surreptitious, therefore the nature of the bow must be decided in a flash. If the situation is such that you are meeting someone who is going to perform a service for you, for example, a bank manager, or a hotel manager, that person's bow will immediately be a deep bow, and yours will be barely a nod.

The *meishi* dance is extremely important to a Japanese gentleman because his entire comportment depends on his stature among his associates in a room, whether the occasion is business or social. Without an exchange of cards, they do not know how to behave, and this is precisely why they are apprehensive when they are invited to a function given by foreigners, who don't carry cards. For the most part, strictly social invitations tend to be refused.

We were also taught a little bit about the nature of the Japanese personality and cultural behavior which we might expect but not understand. For instance, they seem to laugh at very inappropriate times, such as when being told of something sad or a story about bad luck. This is because it is considered to be bad manners to show emotion in public, and I guess that laughing covers up a display of even dismay, let alone grief. Something bordering on grief is only acceptable if it is shown as part of an apology. So great is this humiliation that tears may be shed. Or suicide contemplated.

I studied Japanese every morning with a tutor, and the first phrases I had to learn were those of extreme courtesy and humility. For instance, the word *sumimasen* can mean "excuse me" or "pardon me" or "thank you" or "I'm sorry." This was, of course, a key word to know and use. When I was walking down the street to my tutor's office, I noticed two people walking in different directions, one a man, the other a woman, nodding in recognition, smiling gently, and saying *sumimasen* to each other as they went on their way. This seemed strange to me, as I saw no breach of etiquette that could apply, so I asked my tutor (*sensei* in Japanese) about it. He said it was a form of apology, in case of a possibility that one might offend the other during the course of the day. It's "apology insurance," I thought. This reminded me of a droll friend of ours in Madrid who used to call his hosts before attending a party to apologize in advance for his stupid behavior, thus avoiding the necessity to apologize the day after.

In Japan, it is also inappropriate to show affection in public, particularly between a man and a woman, no matter who they are. This was something new for us after living in Spain where men embrace each other heartily and women kiss both cheeks, and then India, where uniformed policemen walk down the street holding hands.

When you extend a social invitation to a party or dinner at your home, the Japanese guest will arrive late with a gift, such as an expensive bottle of scotch or a silk scarf. In most instances, we found that Japanese individuals accepted our invitations with great pleasure, but with no intention of turning up. We were told that this is because they cannot reciprocate with an invitation to their home, as they would consider their houses too humble . . . as opposed to India, when one of your guests brings his entire family, including cousins, with no advance notice to the hostess.

I specifically remember when I phoned a new Japanese neighbor to invite her and her husband to a Christmas party six weeks later, and she said, "Yes, we will come, but maybe I will have a cold." On the evening of the party, her American husband came alone, no surprise there. At other times when an invitation had been extended to a Japanese coworker of Frank's who was unmarried, he did arrive, but very late and a bit inebriated. False courage.

When I was formally introduced to a Japanese person in English, at a reception for example, the accepted opener of a conversation was the question, "How old are you?" We would consider this to be incredibly rude in the U.S., but in Japan it is not. Age is revered and deeply respected. I found it interesting, when I went to the hairdresser in my neighborhood, that almost all the older Japanese women were having their hair dyed black to cover the gray, because it would be considered impertinent to allow it to turn gray and then expect people to look up to them. Only very old people had gray hair, and, for some reason, celebrities such as artists or movie stars.

Beauty is in the eye of the beholder, and in Japan, the feature considered most beautiful was a large nose. We would look at a Japanese woman with pert features and consider her beautiful, but a Japanese man would look for a large nose. This also applied to men. Whereas an American might push up the tip of his nose to denote the term "snooty," the Japanese might make a loose fist and place it around the nose, meaning "he acts like a man with a big nose" and that he is conceited or full of himself.

The Trains

The Yamanote-sen is the commuter train that runs around the periphery of the city of Tokyo. It is daunting, to say the least. The train station was a short walk from our house, and the first time I bought a ticket, I saw the first train so jammed with people that I decided to wait for another one. I came to realize that the smiling platform conductor who was pushing people onto the train, the way one sits on a suitcase to squeeze it shut, was quite literally a people pusher. That was his job. Everyone was very patient with him. If anyone had fainted on one of those trains, he would absolutely not fall down, because he would be pinned in an upright position by all the other people. I thought I would never get used to it, but after discovering that taxis took hours, I faced the alternative.

Frequently, it was necessary to transfer from one train to another, or to switch to the subway. The first time I switched trains, I mistakenly got into a train on the wrong side of the track. Having absolutely no idea what the names of the stations should be and with signs only in Japanese, I sat on the train for some time, until I noticed that the crowd had thinned out, and that the people still seated were dressed like peasants or farmers. When the view out the window grew decidedly bucolic, I realized that I indeed was a long way out of Tokyo. I was embarrassed to jump up and get off the train, not knowing where I was, but I realized I had to "lose face." It was like a bad dream. I approached a Japanese woman who understood my clumsy Japanese, and not only did she show me where to get on another train, she came with me. We came to find that this was not unusual in Tokyo, in fact, it seemed to be the norm. The extreme courtesy displayed by these people was a joy, not to mention their honesty.

Integrity

One time, Frank returned from the airport in a taxi, and after paying the driver and tending to his luggage, he realized he had left his wallet in the taxi. He had no idea what taxi company it was or how to phone them, so he faced the fact that he was going to have to cancel his credit cards and accept the loss of the money. Our phone rang shortly thereafter. It was a gentleman speaking in Japanese, calling from the airport to say that he had found Frank's wallet in the taxi. He apologized for not being able to return it immediately, explaining that he was about to board a plane, but that he would return the wallet when he flew back on the following Thursday. He even quoted the amount of yen that was in the wallet to ensure that Frank would know that none was stolen. When he arrived at our door in a taxi, the evening of the following Thursday, with Frank's wallet in hand, Frank tried to reward him, but he insisted it was absolutely not necessary and complimented Frank on his ability to speak Japanese.

Insularity

When Frank was asked by his company to give a talk in Japanese to a group of businessmen, he worked with our tutor for several weeks to prepare. He was so apprehensive about making mistakes that he asked the tutor to record the entire speech in his own voice. Frank listened to it over and over, capturing and memorizing every nuance.

On the morning of the speech, Frank felt confident and prepared. When he gave the talk, he felt it went well, and when he concluded, the Japanese businessmen stood and filed out in silence. Frank was devastated. Could it have been that bad? His right-hand man, who was Japanese, reluctantly explained what had happened.

The Japanese pride themselves on the fact that their language is considered to be the most difficult in the world. They have always isolated themselves as much as possible to keep the race pure, and even though there have been mixed marriages, it was usually Japanese women who married foreigners. When a *gaijin* (foreigner) makes a speech in Japanese, using good vocabulary and the proper accent, it is looked upon as an infringement, a penetration of their wall of insulation, and is considered an impertinence. If Frank had made a less polished speech, with perhaps a mistaken pronunciation here and there, or the wrong accent, or even the wrong word, it would have been greeted with broad smiles and nods and compliments, but they would be thinking, "Well, you tried and we appreciate that. It is to be admired, but you don't speak our language well."

Frank told this story to a foreign businessman who had lived in Japan since early childhood and spoke Japanese like a native. He told Frank that he should have deliberately made mistakes, and that by doing so, his listeners would've felt safe.

"With your perfect Japanese, they might even think that you're with the CIA," he said. They both laughed.

In a Crowd

Harking back to our initial impression of Japanese people in foreign countries, always traveling in a crowd, we realized when we lived in Japan that it didn't matter where we went, we were always in a crowd. The Japanese were accustomed to bumping into and being pressed by a throng of humanity, and I wondered if their unflagging courtesy came from the fact that they would kill each other if they resented being pushed. My theory was actually that they felt safe in a pack.

When we went skiing in northern Japan, the crowd on the slopes was downright dangerous. I was never a good skier, and knowing my limitations, I stayed with the baby slopes, but I still fell down. While trying to scramble into a vertical position, I looked up from my crab-like crouch and saw an entire line of Japanese skiers listening to their instructor. After one loud command, all of them started down the hill. Together. I was struck with terror. I was in their way. I started screaming. They were all staring straight ahead, like robots, and I was sure I was facing an ugly death, but the last man in the line passed me as he hurtled down the hill, staring straight ahead, using his poles for speed, the spike of one pole just inches above my head. I was so terrified that after I was helped up, I actually took off my skis and tramped up to the top of the hill. I have never skied since.

One night, we were with our neighbors in their car, driving through a residential area, and I saw a young Japanese man running down the street. "I wonder why he's running," I said, thinking there must be some sort of interesting crisis. "He's hurrying to get into a crowd," Frank said with a smile.

Even when being pinned upright in the train, I was always aware of the courtesy and the silence. Nobody seemed to talk on the train. And most of the Japanese people would read, even while standing and swaying. The phenomenon I noticed was that if this had been a train in Europe, the body odor would have been intolerable. On the Tokyo train, there was none at all. Didn't these people sweat?

Games and Classes

The most important aspect of our life in Tokyo was that our children loved their school and had never had a better time. Plus, they definitely had never been to a better school. This was a school that had hired the smartest and finest teachers available, because it received so many applications. We became active attendees at the kids' school activities. Our children were involved in football, soccer, field hockey, cheerleading, drama, and debate.

Frank and I were genuinely excited about the events our children were taking part in, particularly the football games because so many other parents were there. We made new friends there as we all become apoplectic with enthusiasm, throwing our arms around each other and screaming whenever our boys made a touchdown. I particularly liked the pre-football ritual whenever we played a Japanese university team. Both of the teams would line up, walk to the middle of the field and bow to each other, and then return to the sidelines. When the games were over on Saturday afternoons, the kids would get together in groups and take the train downtown, to see a movie, or go to a disco, or eat at a noodle shop. They were always completely safe. We were spared the worries we had heard about when children become teenagers.

As for classes or groups, well, I was not much of a joiner. Large groups of women always left me tongue-tied and usually bored. I didn't seem to have an ability to even listen to the minutes of a meeting, far less be the secretary. There were a multitude of craft classes I could've taken, such as origami (making butterflies out of pages of a magazine), or macramé (making ugly plant hangers out of rope), or ikebana (Japanese flower arranging). I did give that one a try but when I reached the correct result, I found it to be too rigid, and the angles too sterile. I preferred a teacup full of pansies. I had a friend who had spent some time in a clinic for depression, and she told me gleefully that the patients in the clinic had all these same classes. "That's what they do in the loony bin," she said.

I guess I have never been one of those ladies who "do lunch." I did enjoy my Japanese language lessons, but that was one-on-one with a tutor. For some reason, the Japanese language structure just made sense to me. I was surprised how few other women made any attempt to learn the language. They claimed it would be too hard. Me, I started watching the soap operas on television.

Lessons from the Tube

I discovered, to my delight, that soap operas on afternoon television in Japan were exactly the same as in the United States. I had never actually followed one soap opera, but I found the Japanese plot and presentation not unlike ours. The plot: The husband is a handsome airline pilot who apparently walks around all the time in his uniform. He drives a sport car. When he leaves the airport, he goes to an apartment in a very classy building, where his mistress lives. You know she is his mistress because she is smoking and drinking whiskey in the middle of the day from a beautiful crystal glass. Her apartment is very modern and glossy, and so is she . . . an uptown chick with terrific western clothes, tight and short. She is apparently berating him for something, but I don't have to know why. They are having a spat, and she is no shrinking violet. Then he kisses her passionately, still wearing his cap. After leaving her apartment, the pilot goes to his Japanese-style home, and is greeted by his wife. She is always smiling, speaks in a gentle whisper, and dresses in a kimono. She kneels to remove his shoes. Then she tippy-toes into the kitchen to make tea for him. The pilot speaks in a big, gravelly, macho voice, letting her know who is boss, and she reacts with deep humility, as a good wife should.

Although I didn't understand what they were saying, it was from this show that I learned the sound of Japanese as spoken by a woman. I did understand a few words here and there. My experience has been that when studying a language, the ear is as important as the memorization of words. Japanese women speak with a little lilt, which is very feminine and clear (I was told later that my tutor should have been a woman). In the soap opera, the wife was the epitome of sweetness, while the mistress, though not crass, spoke more directly and even showed annoyance. A good woman and a bad woman.

Being blessed with a good ear, I gradually started to imitate the cadence of the women's voices on television, but I could not speak as wistfully as the wife. I guess I was a bad woman. At first, I used to watch the show while sorting laundry, but ultimately I enjoyed it so much that I started following it. I was surprised at what good actors they were. One wouldn't expect that in a people whose culture dictates that they never show emotion. Perhaps acting served as an outlet. It "scruted" the inscrutable.

Economics

During our ongoing battle against bankruptcy, I became bitter about the sacrifice the entire family had to accept. It was embarrassing that I owned only one fashionable cocktail dress, which I had bought on sale in a downtown boutique. All my other clothes were out of style. We came to refer to this frock as The Red Dress. We hid our budget problems because we were, after all, the family of an affluent businessman—one who didn't have a car "because the train was more convenient."

When Johanna was considering a dress for an upcoming prom, I started to look at formal gowns just to see if it would be at all affordable to get a dress from a shop. It was not possible, so she and I went shopping for a dress pattern and fabric so that I could make the dress. The last time I had used a sewing machine for anything more than mending was when I had made maternity clothes. The dress was a challenge, but it was my personal triumph, and I gave silent thanks to the old-fashioned school system I had grown up with, which deemed that young ladies should know how to sew.

I was tired of being broke. I was tired of the nagging worry, waking in the middle of the night with a core of fear. We had no savings. We had no investments. We actually couldn't afford the college tuition for our kids. We had to deny Kristin her first choice, Stanford University, because we could not afford the tuition. The American International School had proven its excellence, resulting in easy admission to the best colleges for all our children, but we could stretch our bank account just so far. Frank had been brought up middle class, and I had been brought up poor, so Frank never doubted that everything would work itself out and we would all live happily ever after.

One night, Frank came home from the office and with a

very straight face said he had something terrific to show me. He opened his brief case and presented our most recent bank statement, trying not to burst out laughing. We had eight dollars and twenty-nine cents in the bank. I started to laugh hysterically. "Let's get drunk," I said. And so we did. All dressed up.

It was increasingly difficult for Frank to carry ten thousand American dollars in cash in a plain envelope to give to a traitor.

The Night Train

During a period of time when I was became involved with a theater group in Tokyo, it would often be very late when I went home at night. A woman alone in Tokyo was absolutely safe, wherever she was, and I felt no apprehension at all walking to the station or standing in the street to hail a taxi. I usually left the theater in the company of a woman who also lived in my neighborhood, so we tried to avoid the 11:15 p.m. train whenever we could. It was whimsically called "the puker." It was the train that Japanese men took after drinking in a bar with their male colleagues after work. Japanese people cannot hold their liquor, because, as my Japanese doctor explained, their "liver is smaller" than that of a Caucasian, and "doesn't filter as well." Being drunk is perfectly all right in the eyes of the Japanese, the theory being that whatever disgraceful behavior is exhibited, it is because of the liquor and not the man. And vomiting on the train was just a part of being drunk. Either we would see a man on the station platform, barfing his evening away, or (please God, we hope not) he would be the person hanging on the train strap and swaying in front of your seat. Nobody looked at a drunk man. After all, we didn't want to hurt his feelings.

Crossing the platform just to get on the train required a kind of dance to avoid stepping in something distasteful. We probably looked like we were playing hopscotch. There was another situation that could unfortunately arise on crowded trains. In the density of the crowd, a male would find the opportunity to grope a female. Johanna had experienced this a few times and was told by her American friend, who had grown up in Tokyo, about an acknowledged custom, which she was not the least bit hesitant to follow after that. When being grabbed, the woman should grab the man's hand, hold it up in the air, and shout "*sukebe!*" which is the Japanese word for lecher. The man would be found guilty amongst a jury of his peers on the train.

Friends and Parties

On weekends, it was not uncommon for us to find three or four teenagers sleeping in our living room in sleeping bags. The train rides were long, and the kids spent the large part of the weekend together, so they slept over, at one house or another. Once John came home from a weekend with one of his best friends and said, "You and Daddy have to meet Barry's parents. They're really your type. I know you'll like them." I asked him why he was so sure. "Well," he said, "last night they were at a party, and they came home at three in the morning because Mr. Cain wasn't feeling well. And then Mrs. Cain went back to the party." I burst out laughing. Aha.

We invited the Cains to our next party. They were a handsome pair, and they mingled instantly. When they arrived, they told us that they had a previous engagement and couldn't stay long. When Rachel (Mrs. Cain) glanced at her watch, she caught her husband's eye, and they very reluctantly had to leave. I saw them to the door and Philip Cain lingered in the foyer, looking longingly into our living room at our noisy crowd. He said, "By God, I can smell a good party here. I hate to leave!" We liked them instantly, and they became very close friends. We were always the last people to leave a good bash, and when either of us were the hosts, we took it for granted that the four of us would put our feet on the coffee table and enjoy a nightcap while analyzing the evening. Worlds away, we have always remained in touch.

Our friends were enormously varied in background and culture, and we mixed them all up. We pushed the dining room table against the wall, and it would be groaning with good food and a bar that never closed. The music was carefully orchestrated with Spanish guitar at the beginning of the evening while conversation was just beginning, graduating to Sinatra and Dave Brubeck when things warmed up, to Chopin during dinner, when people were sitting on the floor or the stairs, then to music with a beat for dancing when the dining room became the ballroom. All those lonely midnight hours of putting together reel-to-reel tapes paid off.

We became famous for our parties, mixing and matching new people.

One night after a particularly clamorous soirée, when the last people had left and we began clearing the glasses and plates, Frank said, "That was a very good party. I think we got three divorces out of that one." And then, after a tedious party where nothing meshed well, he said, "It should be against the law to be boring." As I began emptying ashtrays, I commented, "I think the prisons would be very crowded," and Frank retorted, "Oh, I wasn't thinking of prison. I think they should be shot."

It wasn't unusual to invite almost 90 people to our Christmas open house. The invitation said "from three p.m. to who knows?" I cooked for a week before, and enjoyed doing it. Frank often said that he would much rather be the host, refilling glasses before they were empty and charming and amusing both women and men. My female friends were always telling me that they were in love with my husband, and I didn't blame them. Here was a man who loved small talk and gossip and flattery. Who wouldn't want to go to his parties? I think I was an accessory, but I didn't mind, because small talk was torture to me. And because cleaning up was Frank's job.

At a particular party, one of our guests, a slight young man who didn't "drink well," decided to leave and go home, a few doors down the street. Frank noticed he was gone, and asked about it. I told him he had gone home. Frank was out the door and down the street, and he returned carrying the laughing young man over his shoulder, saying, "Nobody leaves our parties."

There are some eastern superstitions about certain houses being happy. I think the rooms of our house faced in the right direction, because ours was a happy house. The front door was always open, and when the school day was over young people were noisily arriving, banging up the stairs, three stereos playing in unison. My constant refrain was "Get off the phone!"

Japanese Police

On a corner in every neighborhood there was a police stand, much like what a sentry would have at a gate. This stand was called a *koban* and the two policemen stationed there were indeed sentries. They had a list of all local residents' names and addresses, not to invade our privacy or to badger, but truly to protect. They greeted us whenever we passed the *koban* either coming from or going to the train station. We were glad they were there, five minutes from our house.

There was a period of time when our neighborhood was regularly visited by a "flasher" on his bicycle. One day, as I was leaving the house, one of our neighbors was running toward her house, looking terrified. "I just saw the flasher!" she cried. "I was heading to the dry cleaners and he came zooming around the corner and exposed *it!*" My neighbor went to the *koban* and in the most subtle and vague terms, told the police about this crime. They understood, and in a few days they caught the flasher, and we were saved.

One day, I received a telephone call from the police, saying that they had arrested our son and that he was at the main police headquarters. It was a miracle that I understood that much, without trying to ask why. I called Frank at the office and I caught a taxi and explained to the driver, I thought, where I wanted to go. The driver pointed at the *koban*. I said, in stilted Japanese, "No. Very big building. Farther away. Many policemen." He did take me to police headquarters, but then I was petrified because I had no idea how to find the right department. I just kept repeating my last name and that my son was a *gaijin* and where was he? Another miracle. I found the waiting room and was told my son was "in that room," and that his friend was in another. I was so glad when Frank came in the door.

Frank talked to the policeman, who was very stern, almost nasty, telling Frank that John had attacked an office building with a deadly weapon. Frank had no idea what that meant, but he wouldn't allow us to talk to John. We waited more than two hours. When John was allowed to come out of an interrogation room, he explained to us that he had been with his friend, David, at his family's apartment. David had a slingshot, so they opened the window and started shooting at branches of trees. The apartment was in a high-rise and apparently, they had hit a window of an office building across the street. Although the pellet didn't go through the window, it had hit a corner, creating a cracked spiderweb effect on the tempered glass. The window would have to be replaced.

The sound of the window getting hit, and the look of that spiderwebbed crack, must have frightened people in the office. They apparently had called the police. John told us that six policemen wearing gas masks banged on the door of the apartment, no doubt expecting assassins. The boys were arrested and taken to the police station to be thoroughly interrogated. The police explained to Frank that a formal apology had to be made to the president of the company in the office building, and that a fine must be paid, plus the cost of replacing the window, to be paid by us and by David's parents. The entire episode was conducted very sternly.

Now we had to find someone who could explain how a formal apology was made. Probably on our knees, we thought. Frank asked the advice of a Japanese colleague in his office. His colleague explained that there had been an incident a few years past when Emperor Hirohito stood on his balcony at the Imperial Palace and waved at the people as an annual event on his birthday. Someone in the crowd had shot at him with a slingshot, using a pachinko ball, which hit Emperor Hirohito on the head. Thus a slingshot was in the category of a deadly weapon. (A pachinko ball is a small steel ball used in pinball machines).

The next day Frank and John, dressed in very serious attire, went to the office building. Humbly, very humbly. Frank told me later that they had to apologize to a number of people who held various executive positions. He also said that he had not been prepared for how humiliating it was. They were treated like war criminals, a far cry from the genial bows and smiles he was accustomed to. Arrangements were made between Frank and David's father to replace the window, at an astronomical cost. It was a certainty that beyond our trust in the police in the *koban*, we must show great respect for the police at large. We never did mention that Frank and I questioned if the boys were really aiming at trees.

On one other occasion, when John and Barry and another high school friend were returning from their senior prom in the wee hours of the morning, John decided it would be a good idea to climb up a stop sign and sit on it. Of course, they had had too many celebratory drinks. When the police pulled up, Barry said to John, "Just act natural." When the police took note of the tuxedoes and boutonnières, they laughed and drove the boys home. Having a good time was legal. And we didn't have to buy a new stop sign.

Our Double Life with Finances

We endured a number of hardships in our double life and one of them was dealing with financial issues. For example, one of Frank's colleagues was informed that he was going to be audited by the IRS. It would seem logical that the CIA would intervene and reveal this man's true salary and true employer, and say, "He's one of us. Back off." What? And blow his cover? Our friend went through a week of interrogation and persecution, arguing about a salary he didn't make at a job that wasn't his. Not to mention the deductions and expenses, which were nonexistent.

The one difference, financially, which existed between deep cover officers and those within the embrace of the embassy was that we were given a 10% cost of living allowance—in the most expensive city in the world. Whenever we asked for remuneration of any kind, the answer was "Take it out of your 10%."

This became a standard quote that we used for amusement. One hundred percent of our salary was a joke, and using 10% of it to cover food alone was a stretch. To entertain guests with decent wine at home was hugely expensive. Beef was $36 a pound, and a cantaloupe was $18, and this was in the seventies. I never did know of anyone buying a cantaloupe. The fruit seller offered beautiful gift-wrapping for a melon.

Weekly allowance for the children was, by American standards, very high. Luckily, there were so many sports activities at the school on weekends that we had to consider only the cost of a movie, a cheap meal, and train fare, which added up to twenty-five American dollars. Each.

When to Tell the Children

Telling the children the truth about their father's work was a very sensitive and subjective decision. Some of our cohorts wondered if they should ever tell them. Was it dangerous? Would they tell their friends? But more than anything, would they feel betrayed by the lie? We decided that at age fifteen they would be adult enough to absorb it and understand, and that Frank should be the one to do this. It was his job, not mine.

When John was fifteen, he and Frank went for a walk in the park, and Frank, who was forever tactful, told his story. When they returned from the walk, John went upstairs to his room without saying a word. He stayed up there for some time, playing his guitar. I asked Frank what had happened. He said that he thought it would just take some time for John to digest and accept what he'd been told. After all, it seemed to be a wild tale from a movie, and certainly not anything that could possibly involve his parents. Our son was stunned.

He told Kristin a year later. Johanna wouldn't know until

just before the start of her junior year. I still don't know how hurtful the apparent "living a lie" could be to a child. How much would it frighten the children? Would they think our lives were as dramatic and frightening as those of spies in the movies?

Still, it was a big relief after all that our children had been told, because the sham could be dropped and their cooperation in the lie, which I had been living with alone, helped me. I think that once they became adults, they were proud of their father. I think also that they appreciated and understood the stress we experienced. Mostly, they considered our lives to be exciting.

The Car

When one of our friends in the neighborhood was transferred, he decided to sell his car. It was a very small car and we thought we could afford it, even if we could never fit our three grown children inside. Our neighbor asked very little for the car; he just wanted to get it off his hands. It had been embarrassing taking a train on a rainy night, and arriving at a party wet and rumpled, when everyone else had a car. I remember writing a letter to a friend, excited to tell her about the car. I called down to Frank from upstairs to ask him what kind of car it was. "Never mind describing it to her," he said. "Just mail it with the letter."

When we first moved into that neighborhood enclave, Frank's embassy contact told him about a man who also lived there who was retired from the CIA. He had decided to stay in Tokyo because he liked his cover job and they were glad to have him. We were told never to become involved with him or his wife, which was absolutely silly because he no longer had any connection with the CIA. One night, after we had all been to an outdoor block party, we started walking home at the same time they were leaving, so they stopped by for a nightcap.

"You know, Frank," our guest said, "You really shouldn't be driving that pathetic little car. If you're supposed to be a businessman, for God's sake, drive a big car." What did he mean? It seemed like he knew about Frank. Or did he? Was he implying that we had bad taste, or was he actually saying that the company should have better taste? We couldn't show any reaction except to laugh.

When the Children Move On

During Christmas week, there were a lot of parties held for the returning college kids, who were for the most part freshmen. The richness of their previous experience of attending high school in Tokyo ironically made it difficult to adjust to an American university campus. They had left a very diversified but warm circle, in which all colors and creeds were embraced, and college was a totally new and different environment. In our case, the children had their entire academic experience in foreign schools, with the exception of our year in the Ivy League. The casual pace of university classes was disorienting. High school had been demanding with at least two hours of assigned homework each night. In their senior year, university courses also became an option for which they would be credited. Kristin's grade point average was 4.2. The point-two extra were university credits.

We had no home in the United States, and although we paid federal taxes, and had at one time paid California taxes, we were not eligible for resident tuition and were forced to pay the tuition paid by foreigners. At one time, we had all three children in different universities, and the expense that year was $45,000. This was a great deal more than Frank's annual salary. We were forced to make loans against his life insurance and to borrow from a friend. CIA personnel who worked in the embassy could send their children to the University of Virginia as residents, this being, ostensibly, their home state. We thought this was terribly unfair to us, and when Frank asked about this privilege, he was told that it would "blow our cover."

Frank presented this conundrum to a close and old friend who was a professor at a very good university and knew about Frank's double career. His friend said he wanted to run through our university applications, showing Frank's true salary, and not the inflated, mythical salary on his income tax forms. Although Frank returned every check from the cover company, and drew his real salary from a bank account in an obscure bank, the income tax statement showed the former.

The result of the hypothetical test was that all three of our children would have been entitled to ample grants. Taking into consideration their high grades, the grants would have also been substantial. This was all done anonymously, but Frank decided to present the results to the Washington desk, asking for financial aid. His request was ignored for a very long time, but Frank continued to pressure them for a decision. The decision finally came in. It was "request refused." It was pointed out to us that our rent was paid, our high school tuition had been paid, and we had a cost of living allowance of 10%. These perks were also given to all the businessmen we knew, but their base salary was substantial.

"I guess," Frank said sarcastically, "it's because of all the use we've made of the American highways, the fire department and the U.S. mail service, plus all the public schools that our taxes have been paying for."

When John, our first high school graduate, went away to college, he was not prepared for the culture shock of being in his own country. Imagine an eighteen-year-old who had spent almost his entire life in foreign countries associating with young people of every race, color, and creed, trying to "belong." They could talk about soccer and football, but it was awkward making any reference to his past life . . . "when I lived in Spain," well, la dee da. It elicited strange expressions that clearly indicated he was considered weird. His peers were not interested. Almost all of them had lived in the same state all their lives, and were able to go home for weekends, phone their parents, and stay in touch with their friends from high school, some of who also became their classmates in college. And they all had cars. They could afford them, probably because their parents paid residents' tuition.

When John found that any reference to his past was met with raised eyebrows and indifference, he pretty much stopped doing it. He didn't talk about anything except generalities. His greatest relief was that he was accepted to play on the soccer team. John had approached the coach, who told him that scouts had chosen the new team players during the past year. But they had never sent scouts to Asia, John clarified, so the coach allowed him to scrimmage. The soccer team was made up almost entirely of Spanish-speaking students from South America who became startled when John seemed to know every play they made and was ready for them. "Cuidado con el rubio," he heard them say. (Watch out for the blond guy.) When they switched positions, and John excitedly discussed the plays in fluent Spanish, they were dumbfounded, but enthusiastic about including him. This was his game and his language.

Socially, however, he felt removed and became intensely lonely for home. Home for him was Japan. When Thanksgiving came and the dorms were closed, he had nowhere to go, and the beginning of a deep depression enveloped him. We felt helpless when we received his letters. He was almost physically ill with depression. He didn't fit in. No one understood the feeling of alienation he was experiencing. He was so heavy-hearted that he lost energy to do anything at all. In one letter, he wrote that he wished he could walk in our front door and ask what's for dinner. For parents who lived thousands of miles away, this was heartbreaking, but we could do nothing. When he broke his ankle during his first soccer game, he felt as though he had lost his last contact with reality. He was on crutches for three months.

The following year, Kristin went to university in California and I went with her while she went through orientation. When she and I went to the dorm to look at her room, all the dorm's doors had signs with the names of the students and their hometowns. Almost all of them had California addresses and, of course, Kristin's was "Tokyo." Her dormmates asked her if she spoke Chinese.

As the days passed, she became more and more tense and lost. I ran around buying bedding and plants for her dorm room, and on the eve of my departure, she came to my hotel to have dinner and spend the night with me. On the morning when I had to leave to return to Tokyo, she broke down and sobbed. It was a foggy morning, and I left her sitting on the grass on a hill overlooking the beach, with her head in her arms and her shoulders shaking. I was so sad I could hardly see the road for my own tears. I felt like I was abandoning my child. And I didn't want to go back to Tokyo. I wanted to be able to say what other parents were saying. I had seen family cars pulling up, parents with their daughters, unloading their suitcases, and lamps from their bedrooms, waving and shouting as they left. "Hey, call us tomorrow. We'll see you in a couple of weeks!

Phone if you need anything. Before you know it, it will be Thanksgiving and the whole family will be together!"

At that point, I hated our life.

We later heard from the parents of a boy who had gone to high school with John in Japan. He had felt so displaced in college in California that he had requested to be transferred to an international dorm, where he felt much more comfortable. He had found his peers. And his father's company paid for him to come home at Christmas and again during the summer. There was no point for us in pursuing that. It seemed that everything we had reasonably requested was denied, like dealing with an enemy. It was the CIA against us. It was like a war.

We had been in Tokyo for seven years. We thought when we left Spain that there could never be a station we could love as much, but Japan had been wonderful for all of us. It was particularly joyful because our children had gone through their teens there, without the problems that were expected with teenagers. They met in groups, traveled on the trains together, or spent time at the homes of their friends. We knew they partied, but it was seldom anything to worry about. They knew their teachers well, as did we. Our young people so liked and respected their teachers that when college freshmen came home for Christmas, by the time jet lag had passed, they were on that three-train ride to school to see their teachers. How often does that happen?

Secrets and Lies

It is certainly not a given that a man who has a hotel room in the best hotels in the city will succumb to temptation, but it is true that a wife will think about the situation as wide open to a romantic liaison. When it was so easy, why not?

Although I trusted Frank and had never allowed myself to question his loyalty, there it was the "why not"? This became a serious problem with one of the Agency wives I knew. Her husband was indeed indulging in a red-hot fling. The seed of doubt is easily planted because we already live a life of duplicity. One more little peccadillo wouldn't matter much, would it? Especially if the man was attractive, with a fake passport and a different name. Lying a little was fine, in fact, it was our coat of arms. Where did honor and trust go when we were living under such a cloak that lies became pedestrian? Under the cloak is the dagger.

Sometimes, in Tokyo, when Frank had spent the previous night in a hotel and then gone straight to the office in the morning, he would bring me flowers he had bought at the flower stand on the street near our house on the way home from the station. I found myself reluctant to take them. I would imagine that his face was flushed, or that he was particularly buoyed, behaving as though he had been gone for weeks. "And how's my sweetheart?" he would say, "Did you miss me?" I had seen him the day before. Why would I miss him? Wasn't this the behavior like that of a man who had experienced a joyful illicit liaison? Secrets. Our life was a tangle of lies and secrets.

I wondered if I knew what was true. When he had gone to Hong Kong and brought me a beautiful gold chain, I wondered why. There were times when he would make a tour of Asia, on business, and once I phoned his hotel room late at night, and there was no answer. I expected that he would be in the company of another woman, younger and more attractive than me. I would keep myself awake, to call again at 2:00 a.m. Still no answer. There was a perverse kind of satisfaction that I experienced. It was an "aha!" It proved I couldn't be fooled. I was too smart. Or maybe I was crazy. Did I not love him enough to trust him, or did I love him too much to think I could keep him?

I became obsessed. Was there a beautiful woman in his room, and was that why he wasn't answering the phone? Or was he in *her* room? So many smart young women were also traveling business executives, staying in the same hotels. Having cocktails in the same bar. I would find myself in an agony of suspicion. It was our job to be suspicious. So, he wasn't what he seemed.

Once when Frank and I were staying in a hotel in another city, we ran into an American friend named George, who was traveling on business. It was a joyous surprise to see him board our airplane. He had come from the U.S. and there was so much to talk about. I knew his wife, and particularly liked her. Of course, we made immediate plans for dinner, and he came up to our room immediately after registering at the hotel.

Frank couldn't stop smiling at George. "Hey," he said, "we have to find a pretty companion for George." George said with a smile that he didn't want a companion. He said that I was pretty enough for both of them. Frank insisted. "Just watch," he said. "I can go down to the lobby and pick up an attractive woman in five minutes. Do you want to bet?" I was stunned. Was this an accomplishment to demonstrate to his wife? George just shrugged and smiled, knowing how gregarious and engaging Frank could be. He treated this as a joke as Frank left the room.

Just a few minutes later, Frank returned with a young American businesswoman who was probably in her thirties. He was triumphant. Was I to think this was amusing? I was humiliated. Had he forgotten I was his wife? How long had he been practicing this game? And where had he honed this craft? Just how smooth was he if he could blithely demonstrate this proof of his charm in my presence? I felt like we had been cohorts for such a long time that he didn't look upon me as his wife. We were partners in crime. We were accomplished actors.

On that particular evening, the young woman accompanied us to dinner, and Frank fawned over her as though she were his date. George and I carried on a conversation across the table, and he was clearly uncomfortable with the entire scene, and he told me so. When we left the restaurant, George suggested we all walk back to the hotel, because it was such a lovely evening. Frank cheerfully waved us off and jumped into a cab with "his date." "Why did he do that?" George asked. I certainly didn't have an answer. Frank had definitely crossed the line, but apparently thought that I would accept any game. When I told him how embarrassing the evening had been, he replied that I seemed to have lost my sense of humor.

On another occasion, after a three-week absence while touring Asia with an American business associate, the two of them came bursting in the front door, exuberant. In greeting me, Frank said, "We never want to see another Oriental girl again! Where is my Scandinavian wife?" And he threw his arms around me. I had not really thought about his being with "Oriental girls" on a business trip, but I was beginning to think differently. His associate, Zach, was a handsome and funny lady's man who had recently separated from his wife. For Zach, it was fun and games.

Frank and Zach launched into a "funny" story about a girl who was sitting between them at a bar. Why was she sitting between them? Although Frank was known to be a ladies' man, it was a term that was fondly bestowed, and was not meant to connote womanizer. He was referred to as "David Niven," the charmer. I didn't know if I was still amused.

I honestly began to believe that Frank was using the CIA as

just cause for indiscretion, the evidence of which was carelessly left around: a book of matches from a "girlie" bar (he had to go there with an agent); numerous charges on his credit card from bars and restaurants, with sums astronomical for only one person (a new man he was cultivating as a possible link); an ornate gold chain he suddenly wore around his neck, far too long and ostentatious for his taste (something he picked up in Hong Kong, a real bargain). Was I paranoid? There was always a glib explanation, conveniently having to do with the game of espionage. He seemed never to be at all self-conscious. It was so easy.

Frank confided to me, with great amusement, that one of the other CIA men in his group was going to "love hotels" in Tokyo, because his agent wanted to go. Frank thought this was amusing. I was not amused (but hey, it's part of the game!). Frank and I had become pals. I had become one of the guys. I had never learned the rules to that game, the rules seeming to be that a CIA officer can indulge in any kind of naughty behavior in the name of the job. Frank was enamored of the game he played, as though it wasn't real, and he was winning. He felt no guilt. His fake passport was carte blanche, and after all, didn't we go the same spy school? Where had I been when they taught betrayal in our personal life? Had I become a wink and a nudge?

In our little neighborhood in Tokyo, there were people from every walk of life. We were advised by the embassy when a young CIA agent moved into the neighborhood that it would not be prudent to socialize with him. Then, one night when we were playing bridge and gossiping with a couple who lived across the street from him, they said he had been seen using the phone booth on the corner of the street, just two doors down from his house. The obvious conclusion was that he was indulging in some extramarital hanky-panky, or he would be using his own phone, right? The gossip was demeaning to his wife, but we could not defend her. Frank too had once used that phone to arrange a meeting . . . thus obscuring the record on our phone bill. He never used that phone booth again.

An intelligence officer with whom we were acquainted, but did not like very much because of his aggressive and overbearing manner, had been married three times when we met him at age forty. Such was his paranoia that he had begun brandishing a gun in his home, terrifying his children with it, threatening them. He was a clever man, a linguist and supposedly a charmer, though I failed to notice the latter. It would be presumptuous to assume that the nature of his work was the reason for his suspicions and his rage, with physical attacks on his wife and children, but it did create a fertile climate within which his actions might be explained. When he married his fourth wife, he was reported to the Agency for beating her, breaking her jaw, and beating and kicking his young children. It was his wife who reported him. By then, he was eligible to retire.

Time to Transfer . . . Again

One afternoon, Frank was summoned to a meeting and was told that a request had been received to have him transferred to South America. It had been a personal request from a case officer who knew him. The case officer said he particularly needed Frank because of his experience and his fluency in Spanish, which was paramount. When Frank told me, I was heartsick. Although I knew we had been lucky to stay in Japan this long, our concern was for Johanna. She was now a junior in high school. Graduating with the friends she had had for seven years was a celebratory event we couldn't expect her to miss. She had been in three different schools before she was ten. Couldn't we request compassionate evaluation of this?

Even if they insisted that Frank be moved, we discussed the possibility of allowing Johanna to stay in Tokyo. Immediately, three families who knew her well offered to have her stay with them, room and board. Although we would miss her, we thought this would be best for her. One of the host families lived next door to us, and our children came in and out of our front doors as though they were family.

Frank asked his superiors if it would be possible to delay our move for a year, and expectedly, they said that would not be possible. Then he asked them about the possibility of paying tuition in Tokyo, rather than South America, for Johanna, as we had found that the tuition would be the same. The answer was no. "If there is a recognized American school in the area in which you reside," that was where she must enroll. Why? Because those are the rules. Our child's fulfillment, her psyche, her happiness was not their concern. We must do what the manual says.

This was the place where I had found home. And even a neighborhood, for the first time in my adult life. I was able to run next door to get a quick bottle of Chardonnay when I had last minute guests, to have someone look in on me when I had the flu, to call each other and meet on the street when a typhoon had blasted through. This was where we waved our flashlights around the house after an earthquake, and seeing the arcs of the same light next door with the sounds of foreign accents calling out, "Are you all right?" It takes time to love, to trust, to sympathize, and for all of it to be real.

I felt like I didn't have the stamina or the emotional reserve to be "new" again, nor did I have the patience and time that's required to invest in new friendships. Where is the guarantee that new friendships will mean anything? Friendship is often happenstance. What are the chances that in the next foreign city, your neighbor will knock on the door and in fifteen minutes you like her. That happened to me in Tokyo. She had a small child with her, and she said, "My husband made me come over. I'm really not into neighbors." "Neither am I," I said. She came in for coffee and one of my most valuable and enduring friendships was born. We used to get the children off to school on dark, rainy mornings, go back to bed, call each other and talk for an hour, cackling with laughter, or listening to each other's troubles. With friendships like these, I was safe. Now I had to go away. Would I feel safe again?

I was so stricken with grief that I enrolled in a group therapy class to talk about my terrible regret at leaving the place which I had grown to love, and even more, leaving the friends I was so close to, and so reluctant to give up. I came away from my group therapy with something valuable that I learned. I wasn't losing my friendships. I was just being separated from my friends. Their love would always be a part of me, and we would try to treasure and preserve that love forever. I would simply have numerous friends all over the world, and always know how rich they had made me.

Many years later, at the bleakest time of my life, when I thought my heart had completely broken and there was no comfort anywhere, I was embraced by five different friends who came to stay with me. They were all friends that I had made in Tokyo. Each of them required a journey. These were now my friends from all over the world.

The Summer of My Discontent

Frank had to start working with a different cover company

for his new station in Venezuela. Once again, we had to tap dance around the questions and details about why and how this change in career was taking place at Frank's age, which was nearing fifty. It is unusual and generally imprudent for a man to leave a job as a successful executive to take a risk not only with a new job, but a job that would require him to open a one-man office in a field he didn't know.

We had to explain that Frank would be moving to New York for a few months and that I would be unable to move with him, because our children were still in college and had summer jobs in California (which was true). I rented a house in California for the summer to be with the kids.

That was the summer of my discontent. I was overwhelmed with uninvited teenage-nearing-twenty guests. They were everywhere, and I knew they were smoking pot . . . "just a passing phase." I was constantly worried and very lonely. I seemed to have become a den mother, but preferred to be a prison warden. Frank had a hotel apartment in New York, and he and his new cover company boss turned out to be soul mates. They were planning on a trip to Venezuela, first-class. In the meantime he was going to upscale parties and making the unbelievable mistake of calling me from those galas. "Hi, sweetheart, guess where I am? I'm at Ted Turner's apartment. I wish you could see it." I could hear the noise and music, and the voice of someone talking to him and his laughing response while I was clearing plates from dinner, elbow-deep in dishwater, and not in a good mood. "Does Ted Turner know you're running up his phone bill?" Then I said something curt and horrible and hung up. I added tears to the dishwater.

Frank had to leave for New York a month before the movers came to our house in Tokyo. I stayed until the school year was over and until Johanna had gone to the prom. Once again, our cover company had been understanding and generous, giving me and Johanna adjoining rooms so she could have her friends over. I allowed Johanna an illicit bottle of champagne to share with them before the prom. That was actually a pleasant time for me, meeting my friends for dinner or drinks. I wished I had the capacity to live in the moment, without dreading what was going to happen next. Did other women know how to accept today's pleasure, knowing it was secure, I wondered? I seemed to live with constant apprehension, always stuck in a time warp, which was never in the now, but in the difficult tomorrow, and the unknown.

The responsibility for the children was always mine. I provided the discussions and comfort every time we moved, the sympathetic ear for the heartbreaking loneliness for which I had no cure, the assistance on applications to universities, and the physical assistance with their actual moves to college. It was always problematic, the physical responsibility for packing and moving and unpacking and staying, with short interludes in between. I felt I was constantly on a tightrope and wasn't sure there was a net. I wished that Frank would say he would be my net, but he didn't have time. I was sentenced to be the pillar around which our family leaned. I didn't have enough strength for it any more. I felt the rebellion, but took no action. There was no choice.

I was very tightly wound during that summer and felt that the weight was too heavy to carry. I knew I had to get away for a few days, so John, Johanna, and I took a drive to Santa Barbara to visit a dear old friend. I wanted to sit on her deck and listen to her husband and John playing their guitars. We sat outside, drinking vodka and tonics and listening to good jazz. My hands began shaking so badly that I couldn't hold my glass. Then I felt my legs start to shake, as though I were experiencing a seizure. At first I tried to hide it, but my entire body was shaking. I interrupted the conversation. "I, I . . . I don't know what's happening to me." They all looked at me and immediately saw what was happening. John grabbed one arm and tried to hold it steady, while my friend's husband raced to get the car.

They took me to the emergency ward of the local hospital. The interns took one look at my shaking body and immediately decided I was a drug user, leaving me on a gurney in the waiting room, until John demanded that they look at me. I was terrified that I was having a stroke, although I wasn't sure what those symptoms would be.

I had been aware of my shaking hands for some time. I was unable to light a cigarette without using both hands to hold the lighter. Now I felt that my entire body was out of control, as was my life. I was given Valium, and was referred to a neurologist the next day. He recommended that I have a CT scan at UCLA Medical Center. Days later, as I drove alone in my rented Pinto, entering the parking lot of the medical center, I felt lost. I shouldn't have to do this alone. My stiff upper lip made people think I was never afraid, so nobody offered to come with me. I needed my husband.

I had always known that the job came first. Frank was an overachiever, intent on making a smashing impression on every person he met, from secretaries to executives, poets to priests. They were all dazzled. When my friend called to tell Frank about my seizure, he expressed concern and asked her to be sure to call him. What I wanted him to say was, "I'll be on the next plane. Tell her not to worry. I'm on my way." But in our strange world, he couldn't do that. He was immensely proud of the fact that I didn't need hand holding. These were the grounds upon which we built the family structure. Problem?

Ask Mama, she'll figure it out. A brain scan was just another family problem that I could deal with. He was blind to the fact that I was afraid and that I felt very alone almost all the time. I felt that at this point in our marriage, he took everything for granted, primarily my independence and strength. That was a sham. I was five years old again.

The scan showed that I had atrophy of the right frontal lobes of the brain, but it "was nothing to worry about." The neurologist said it would gradually affect my short-term memory. But it had nothing to do with my seizure. The doctor kindly suggested that moving to a foreign country was probably ample cause for what he described as a "terrible anxiety attack." I carried Valium with me at all times. I didn't want to be a scaredy-cat. Not me.

Miami and Visas

When Frank joined us in California for the trip to South America, we could only go as far as Miami because apparently the CIA had neglected to process our visas. It wasn't anything that we would even we have thought about, because we were in our own country, and we thought securing visas would be simple. It was an oversight.

We were instructed to find a motel in Miami until we heard from higher-ups. Our primary concern was for Johanna. We hoped that we would arrive in Venezuela well before the opening of the high school year, which was fast approaching. Frank was peppering Washington with calls, explaining the urgency, but nothing happened. I asked Frank, what if we went to Venezuela without the necessary visas? Would it be logical that Johanna enroll in school? We both decided to go there as tourists. Thus, Johanna could start school. This meant, however, that Frank would not be able to open an office, nor would I be expected to look for an apartment. This also meant that we would have to leave the country later, to apply for the proper visas.

Johanna was eager to get to Venezuela. I understood. Personally, I could not stand one more breakfast with the old people shuffling in, the old men wearing shorts with knee-high socks and wing tip shoes and fedoras, their wives all in pastel-colored aerobic suits, staring at each other with acrimony. The previous evening, the elderly piano player had dropped dead of a heart attack while playing. "After You've Gone."

Here's the breakfast repartee we overheard:

"So, Morris. What are you going to do today?" "Mildew," he replied. These people were depressing. Mildew was now a verb.

A few more days passed and Johanna's school in Venezuela began classes, which meant she was already late. We decided to go to Venezuela and simply tell the truth about our visas, explaining that "red tape" held us up. Red tape covers anything. This way, we could also discuss Frank's career plans with people, and it would be natural to look around for possible office space and an apartment.

Venezuela (1981-1982)

The Welcome Wagon

We arrived in Venezuela very early in the morning, and took a taxi to the hotel apartment where we were told to stay temporarily. What we saw on the drive from the airport was shocking. There were hilly areas with decrepit old shacks and clearly wretched, smelly conditions. This was entirely unexpected. This was a rich country that had been described by the government bureau as beautiful, with a perfect climate like "eternal spring." This was not to be compared with our airport drive into New Delhi, however. There, the misery was upon us, an assault of homelessness coming in the windows, masked with smiles. The vista in Venezuela was like a watercolor painting when you looked "up there," as in, not near the road. A demarcation: them and us. We were all tired on that drive, and remained silent.

When we arrived at our hotel apartment, Frank and I stood on the tiny concrete balcony overlooking other apartments, and while standing there we had to jump back to avoid some disgusting spillage from above. When we looked across at other apartments, we could see that they were throwing their garbage over the balconies into the stairwell. I started to cry. "Why did you bring us here?" I wailed. "How could we do this again?" I hated this place, I hated Frank, and I hated the CIA.

I wanted to run away. I couldn't withstand another horrifying experience like India.

We were entering an era that would be hard on our marriage. I could feel it. I was seething with bitterness. We had actually tried to avoid another move anywhere, because Frank would be eligible for retirement in a year. I could not be consoled. It didn't matter, because Frank made no move to comfort me.

We tried to find a bright side to our situation and went to the hotel dining room to enjoy the buffet, the tropical fruit, and the new spicy dishes we had never tasted. It wasn't until later, when Frank met his embassy contact, that we learned we were not allowed to eat at that restaurant because we had no food allowance. We had to pay for our meals ourselves, and I was expected to shop for groceries and cook in the suite, which had a kitchenette. That certainly cheered me up.

I found it strange that we were in a "brand name" hotel, and that it was located in the center of such squalor. I deduced that the whole city must be pretty much like this, but that wasn't the case. It turned out that this was the only hotel with kitchenettes, and much cheaper than the beautiful hotel in a verdant, residential area where other executives always stayed. The other hotel was where Frank had stayed when he had traveled here with his cover company boss.

Frank was now representing a Park Avenue firm, so it was a glaring mistake to have to admit that this company had put us there. When the cover company later discovered where we had stayed, the president was indignant. It reflected upon him and his company. He was an extremely urbane, sophisticated man, to whom this lack of style was an embarrassment.

There was a small grocery attached to the hotel, but not a part of it. When I walked in the door and smelled the wafts of fresh-killed meat, my past in India came flooding back.

My greatest shock was the price of food. It was higher than in Tokyo. Was this possible? I assumed it must be because they had captive customers from the hotel, but this was not the case. I later discovered that this city was more expensive than Tokyo in every respect. During our entire one year there, we had dinner in a restaurant once. And I didn't buy one article of clothing, or even a lipstick.

The School in Venezuela

Our pressing concern was to immediately enroll Johanna in school, as classes had already started a week earlier. We took a taxi to the international school from our hotel and I was once again speechless. The drive to the school took us through dirty pueblos on gravel-and-dirt roads riddled with huge potholes, and shabby people grinning weirdly at us as we drove by. Were these the slums? It was frightening. To me, their grins seemed menacing, as if to suggest, "I'll get you later." Would I ever dare drive these roads alone? (I did.) I had the same feeling in the pit of my stomach that I had always had in New Delhi. I was repulsed by these particular surroundings, and I felt fear.

The school was a tattered display of run-down buildings, beginning with a row of lockers for the students, which were broken and bashed, nearly every one of them. It was as though marauders had hit the school the night before. My mouth was agape. Johanna was impassive. She was handling this better than I.

Since school was in session, Johanna's walking the halls with her mother and the admission counselor only made her stand out as the new girl. Groups of students all watched and whispered as we walked by or peered into classrooms already in session. After hearing about Johanna's interest in drama, the counselor took us to see the theater. She opened the door and waved her hand like Vanna White displaying a prize. The theater was a dark little hole with broken seats and a stage that was nothing more than a space in front of the seats. The theater at the school in Tokyo had been large, modern, and equipped in every way for a professional production. I wanted to take Johanna's hand and run. I had not yet been informed that nobody could leave the country without a government permit, whether for a short-time absence or a final departure. We were prisoners.

When talking to the admissions counselor, we made enquiries about a school bus stopping at our hotel to pick up Johanna and drop her off. We were told that the bus did not pick anyone up in that district. It was too dangerous. Jesus. We discussed the possibility of hiring a taxi driver to take Johanna to school and pick her up at the end of the school day, at our own expense. It seemed to be our only solution. I felt I should scheme to go with Johanna and sit at the front gate of the dirty yard of the school with a whip.

Johanna showed enormous grace and a lot more class than her mother. This applied to our entire stay in Venezuela. Even when the taxi driver forgot to pick her up at school, this sixteen-year-old seemed to be able to handle anything. I had always been proud of her, but never as proud as I was then. Meanwhile, I sniveled and bitched about everything in general. This school was not the same as the American School in Tokyo and I wondered how they got away with telling us that it was. How did our government describe this disgrace of a school in their handy little manual?

On the second or third day Johanna was in school, she found her locker had been smashed and her personal belongings stolen. Why was it necessary to bash the locker? I was angry but

Johanna didn't want to discuss it. I bitterly complained about our circumstances and she ended up consoling *me*. Again. One night, I thought I could hear her crying in her bed. My first instinct was to go into her room to comfort her, but she was displaying such dignity that I didn't want to intrude.

A week into our stay at the hotel, Frank befriended the general manager who was a delightful man from Chile and spoke Spanish clearly. He lived in an apartment like ours, though not as bare. He invited us over for drinks and during the course of our conversation we discovered that his wife had not been out of the apartment for months. She had developed agoraphobia. Her husband told us that he had been begging for a transfer to another hotel for a long time, and that if he didn't get one, he planned to resign. His wife was a beautiful, educated woman. Smart enough not to go outside, I thought. It turned out that they had a son who also attended the international school and was taken to school by their driver. When we told them about Johanna, the manager graciously offered to have Johanna join their son in their car. There was another new student staying in the hotel as well. They'd all carpool together.

A Furnished Apartment

I was desperate to get out of that area and away from the smelly little store. I felt it was imperative that I start apartment hunting immediately. As we were not allowed to ship our furniture to Venezuela, my choices were limited to furnished places. I was referred to a rental agency run by a young man who had been educated in the United States and was extremely accommodating. When I was taken around the city to look at furnished apartments to lease, I was struck by the natural beauty of the setting, the hills, the tropical greenery, the sprawling houses with grand verandas. Ignoring the dirt and the shambles that was called downtown, I felt a glimmer of hope. Downtown traffic was screeching chaos, with cars actually driving on the sidewalk, traffic lights and signals being totally ignored, and everyone blasting the horn. The majority of the cars were dented and smashed, which was no surprise, except for the town cars with hired drivers.

There were beautiful areas where all the rich people lived, and I decided to be one of the rich people. I was buoyed and impressed by the furnished houses and apartments that I had seen, but they were beyond our price range. The balmy air was indeed redolent of spring. There were beautiful views and balconies wild with foliage. I could see that we might be lucky enough to find such a place, which would divorce us from the circus below.

I was determined to find a place with a view . . . and I did. It was a penthouse apartment with private access to the roof terrace. From the bedroom, a window overlooked a huge soccer field across the street. The owner of the apartment said that the field was used very infrequently and would not disturb us. From the balcony off the living room, there was a view of a verdant golf course and its clubhouse, and beyond that, green hills and mountains. The apartment itself was tastefully and simply furnished, in pale colors. The living room was light and airy and open to the breezes, and a small circular stairway led to the roof terrace. The kitchen was bright and well equipped. We loved this apartment.

The German owner of the building had immediate plans to leave for Brazil and was in a hurry to lease the unit. She told us that someone else was interested in the apartment, and to claim it, we would have to pay $9,000 up front. Due to the fact that we still had no work visas, it was necessary for us to pay the money and do the negotiating. This should have been undertaken by Frank's cover company, but in our current category as tourists, our commercial connection could not be revealed. The CIA provided us with the funds. I was genuinely optimistic now that I had seen the other side of the mountain, as it were.

When we moved in, we were each given a set of five keys to access our sunny, breezy apartment. We had more keys than a prison warden: one for the front gate, one for the door of the main building, one for the private elevator that went directly into our living room, one for our apartment's front door, and one for the garage. I was actually glad we had no furniture. This way we could make a quick getaway, like con men.

As we were settling in, it dawned on us that we hadn't seen any mailboxes. We wondered if the concierge distributed the mail, but that seemed improbable. Then I thought back to other apartment buildings I had looked at, and I could not remember seeing mailboxes, nor had I ever seen a post office anywhere, or a mailman on the street. The puzzle was explained to us later. There was no post office. Therefore, there were no mailboxes. It was unbelievable.

The Noise

On the first day of our stay in the apartment, a soccer game began below our bedroom window. Starting at 8:00 a.m. successive soccer games began, complete with roaring fans, bells and whistles. The games went on all day, almost without intervals. It turned out to be *the* soccer field for the entire country, for every school, every college, and every major league. This was our introduction to The Noise.

When we sat on our beautiful balcony by the living room,

enjoying the view, it was impossible to have a conversation, because of The Noise. Our lips moved, but the sound was drowned out by unbelievable traffic cacophony. It was much worse than New York City. We soon found out that anyone could purchase police sirens anywhere, and this accessory seemed to be the rage. The very rich of this city apparently also collected cars. One tenant in our apartment building had six cars in the garage. I think they had worked out a system whereby they could manage to have all the cars on the road at one time, all with horns blaring. I was sick with regret that I had not returned to the apartment at different times of the day because I should have been suspicious of the soccer field. After talking to people who lived in other areas, I was relieved to know that except for the soccer games, the traffic noise was unbearable: everywhere. People in apartments simply didn't open their windows, which muffled The Noise slightly. It seemed that this city was famous for its noise. Frank said he had thought Cairo was the runner-up.

On the day that Venezuela won the soccer championship, the blaring of horns and the screaming of people hanging out of windows or through sunroofs of cars went on all night. Frank and I roamed the apartment, looking for a place where we could talk, but even in the bathroom, we were overwhelmed by The Noise. I wondered if the German owner had paid someone off to prevent a soccer game while I was looking at the apartment.

The Pep Talk

A friend had given us the name of a man who was American and who had lived in Venezuela for a long time. While we were living in the hotel, we contacted him, and he generously invited us to his home for dinner. I could have fallen on my knees with gratitude. He even came to pick us up. He was from Texas, with the expansive good nature we had found in Texans wherever they are. His wife was a native Venezuelan who did not have an American passport, and her government denied her right to leave the country, offering no apparent reason. She was away and visiting her sister on the evening we were there. He stood behind his bar making rum drinks. "I hate this place," he said, "and I don't apologize for it. I'll always hate this place. Everyone does. You will, too." He handed us our drinks. We both took a long pull of the strong rum.

"There is total corruption here," he went on, "and the people you must fear the most are the police. Always carry at least a hundred dollars of American cash to give to the police when they stop you . . . and they will stop you . . . and don't argue, ever. And never let them in your house because they'll case the place and send somebody to rob you. Don't wear any jewelry, either. Put jewelry in the bank . . . and be careful of security guards. They'll rob you too."

When I asked how a security guard could rob us, I was thinking of the security guard that stood at the gate to our apartment building. "That's easy," he said. "He just might tell you that he won't always let your pretty daughter in the gate. You're not going to take a chance on that, are you?" It was he who explained how we could send and receive mail.

An enterprising American had started an airmail service out of Miami. On a chartered plane, this service would fly letters and parcels to a post office box in a particular building downtown. There was a monthly charge for this service, and we looked into it both for our personal mail and Frank's business address, after he found an office. It was like the mail service in the military, with an APO Box in Miami.

Setting Up the Office

Frank found office space in a centrally located building which, coincidentally, was also where the mail service was set up. He was supposedly opening a new branch of a company emanating from a very good address in New York. This meant that his office should be well appointed. It was going to be an expensive venture. Frank and I worked together on the furnishings, and found very good-looking things on sale at a furniture store that was closing. The cost of good furniture was unbelievably high. Still, the CIA was appalled at the expense. It appeared that there had never been a deep cover man in Venezuela, living on the economy, and the man Frank was replacing had worked within the embassy. The Agency bean counters behaved as though we were trying to make a profit, as if it just wasn't possible for furniture to be so expensive. And it was on sale! I sometimes wondered if embassy people looked at a local grocery store in order to be properly shocked . . . and grateful.

Earlier I had become friendly with the wife of the manager of our hotel, and went to have tea with her one day. I expressed my admiration for a woven tapestry on the wall. She told me it came from Peru, and that a stewardess friend of hers had transported it. If I wanted, she would be glad to ask her friend to buy another one for me. I was enthusiastic about buying a tapestry, so I prepaid for the purchase. When I received it, I was delighted. It was very large, a piece that would cover a wall and definitely be the focal point of the room. Unfortunately, it didn't fit in with the decor of our apartment, because the decor was minimalist and modern, and the tapestry was earthy, woven with heavy wool. Frank liked it and asked if he could hang it in his office, which seemed like a good idea. Otherwise, it would just be stored in a closet until a later date. After we put up a few paintings, the office looked extremely smart; definitely the kind of office his cover company would approve of.

It was going to be dicey hiring a secretary. Frank's work hours had to be flexible, or it would be clumsy to explain his activities to a secretary. The salary of a bilingual secretary who also worked as a bookkeeper was also far more than the budget allowed. We were faced with the only solution: I would be Frank's secretary. We thought it would work, because Frank and I got along extremely well, but it was a prickly situation. In this circumstance, there would be very little actual business transacted, and the facade was all that mattered. It was also a perfect place for the representative in the embassy to drop in on Frank to arrange his meetings. The emissary from the embassy was complimentary about the office and admired the tapestry. He was very capable and experienced, and spoke Spanish like a native, which made things easier for Frank. I had the distinct feeling that he looked askance at my presence. I was paid a thousand dollars a month, which was a bargain, but we could use that money for corn flakes and other luxuries. We did tend to be testy around embassy personnel because our experience had not always been pleasant.

Our Social Life

After we moved from the hotel into our new apartment, Johanna was picked up by the school bus at the front gate. It was interesting to note that most of her new friends were the Spanish-speaking Venezuelans, rather than Americans passing through. This was a natural inclination for Johanna, since Spanish was her first language. She started bringing friends home, and I could hear the laughter from her bedroom. The roof terrace was ideal for her to have her friends over in the evening, and we could hear them dancing to the portable stereo. It was a perfect arrangement for Frank and me as well, once again recognizing the safety of having Johanna home, and yet having our own privacy, sitting on the living room balcony defying The Noise.

When the fall play was announced, Johanna auditioned for it and got one of the leading roles. It was amazing and wonderful to see how that changed things. The other cast members became her friends and her circle of friends grew wider. Then, in the spring, auditions were held for *Peter Pan*, and she was cast in the leading role as Wendy. During rehearsals, other students would drop in to watch, and she became a celebrity of sorts. My most important wish had come true. Johanna was happy.

Frank and I also had great luck meeting "our types" of people. I met a European man at the apartment rental office who seemed very nice—and good looking. I always like that in a man. We exchanged phone numbers and he and his wife soon became a "must" couple in our social calendar. Then Johanna arranged to have her friend's parents sit with us at her fall play, because she knew we'd like each other. They were gregarious and humorous . . . add them to the list. Then there was the British couple that lived in our building and was also very charming, as were Australian friends of theirs. Add the hotel manager and his wife. Mix well. The ingredients made for a good party. Our social life flourished. I loved our apartment and it was eternal springtime.

The Meetings

Frank was to take over an ongoing agenda of clandestine meetings that had been handled by the man who preceded him. He did not have an official meeting with the chief of station, but he was introduced to him. A liaison officer from the embassy would meet with Frank at our office. Frank's agent meetings could be arranged at a coffee shop or at hotels, and the modus operandi here was that Frank did not spend the night at the hotels. He carried a small tote bag, checked in, and after the meeting return home. Then he would return to the hotel in the morning, pay the bill, and check out. We had no idea why it was done this way. Perhaps because he always registered in small hotels in obscure areas of the city ...? It was probably considered too clumsy to go to the big hotels and take the chance of running into people who knew him. The large hotels there offered memberships for use of their pools and tennis courts, so people we knew might easily be there on a daily basis.

It was not Frank's place to argue about the set-up of an operation that had been ongoing for some time. In a way, it made life simpler. For the first time, Frank actually found his job boring. After Frank had one meeting with an agent, which was set up by the embassy, he came home and said that he really wanted me to see this guy. When I asked him why, he said, "You'll see." He went on to say that the meeting was to be in a very public place, in a shopping mall that was "open air" with a number of mezzanines that had small tables and chairs. I believe they are described as "ice cream chairs," in other words, very small. "I told them," Frank said, "that I thought this was a bad idea, because it's the most popular mall in the city, but they said so what, you could be having coffee with a business client. Nobody will notice you."

The next time he was to meet with this man, Frank suggested that I just walk by and glance at them, so I would know what he meant by "you have to see this guy." At the appointed time, I saw Frank sitting at a little white table, with a man whose back was to me, but who was so grossly obese that his buttocks were literally hanging over the side of the chair. He weighed at least three hundred pounds. I caught Frank's quick glance as I passed, and saw the man's face. He was seriously cross-eyed, but not with eyeballs crossing toward each other. Both eyeballs were rolling all over the place. Now there was a man nobody would notice.

Robbery

Frank and I had a great time during our stay in Venezuela. It was the same kind of camaraderie we had found in India. All of us were waiting for the *cedula*, the government pass to leave the country. It was something like parole. Each time a foreigner left the country, whether for a vacation or a business trip, the application for a *cedula* had to be made. Comically, it did seem like they were trying to keep the inmates in prison. Our Texan friend was right. Everyone hated the place, not just because it was unpleasant, but because the corruption was total, and we were honestly afraid, even the men.

Once again, we had a tiny little car, the purchase of which was made by the cover company. I could park it anywhere. There was a local market for groceries, and that was as far as I would go. This market was much more pleasant than the hotel market and had more variety. Frank never went to the market because he didn't like the strong smell of the meat, but I became accustomed to it. When I returned from my drive to the market, I asked Frank to meet me in the garage, so he could be there while the gate to the street closed behind me. It closed from side to side and seemed to take forever.

We attended a dinner party once that was in a lovely home with a gorgeous patio. It was a balmy evening with a slight breeze. There were several small tables with pink tablecloths, flowers, and candles. Servants in uniforms darted about. Cocktails were served outdoors. We commented on what a beautiful evening it was, and I felt optimistic. Everyone looked tan and handsome.

When we sat down to dinner, I found myself seated at a table for six with interesting people I hadn't met before, one of them being a German woman who was talking about her experiences since moving there with her husband. She said that at a dinner party much like this one, with tables outdoors, the guests were accosted by a trio of armed robbers demanding their jewelry. She said she refused to give up her wedding ring. Then she showed me her ring finger, which was hugely scarred and without a ring. The thief had taken a knife from his pocket and said he would cut her finger, and he started to do just that, removing flesh, when she screamed and gave him the ring. I found this story horrifying, and from that date, I never again wore my wedding ring or any other jewelry in Venezuela.

The method of robbery most often described to me was that a robber pulled up beside your car at a red light, usually on a motorcycle, and reaching into the window ripped off your necklace or gold chains. Keeping the windows rolled up seemed like a good idea. It had never occurred to me that we could be robbed so readily at a dinner party in a private home. Although I was impressed by the home, I was glad we lived in an apartment with all those keys.

Staying Alive on Venezuela's Roads

To drive in downtown traffic, it helped if you were insane. It truly was not unusual to see a car jump the curb and drive down the sidewalk at a high speed, in order to pass, and the sound of horns and yells were a constant. I was warned to cover up my fair hair when I went out, to avoid being accosted by men, and always to keep the windows of my car closed and door locked.

Frank drove the car to his meetings. One evening he had a meeting at the Hilton Hotel, and on the way, he stopped to get gas. When he got back into the car, he noticed that the front license plate had fallen off. He got out, picked it up and put it on the front seat. As he was about to pull away, two policemen stopped him. They had seen what happened, but nevertheless told Frank he was driving illegally without a front license plate. One policeman sat in the back seat, and one in the front. The one in the backseat leaned over and twirled his gun near Frank's ear. Corny, but effective. It wasn't until later that Frank realized he should never speak in Spanish, and should pretend to misunderstand when approached by police. We had, however, taken the advice of the Texan, and had a hundred American dollars in cash at all times.

The police told Frank they would have to impound the car, and that it might be difficult for them to remember where it was impounded. They also said they probably would have to take away Frank's international driver's license. When he showed them the American cash, they said it really wasn't enough for both of them, but it would have to do. They did not even pretend that they were legit and going to turn the money over to the police department. They then asked Frank to drive them home to two different locations. It sounds naive on their part to reveal their home locations, but it didn't matter. They knew that neither Frank nor anyone else would report them. To whom?

A popular place for the police to stop cars was on the road to the airport. If anyone was driving to the airport, there was a time limit involved, either to catch a plane or to pick someone up. Thus there was very little discussion and everyone carried cash to the airport. Although this did not happen to us, we were once stopped in city traffic by a policeman who said we had run a red light. There were no traffic lights on that street, but we didn't protest and pretended we didn't understand Spanish. A small piece of paper was handed to Frank through the window, on which was written simply "$100." A nice, round figure. We gave him the money and carried on. "Do you think I can put this on my expense account?" Frank asked. "Take it out of your 1070," I said. We couldn't stop laughing.

We had experienced corruption and thieves in India, but at least they were in our employ, or in business, so we didn't actually live in fear. Here, we lived in fear.

The Vigil

After we had been in Venezuela for a few months, Frank said he could not see the reason why he'd been singled out for this posting. All the agents he handled were already in place and there was no reason to recruit new ones. He couldn't figure out why they had specified they needed a man with experience for this sensitive posting. Any intelligence officer who could speak Spanish would have been capable of handling the situation. And I was still the translator at large, whenever written reports were given to Frank. I did this at home, on my bouncy little Brother's portable typewriter.

One night, Frank had a meeting in a small hotel with an agent. Per usual, I expected him home no later than 11:00 p.m. Johanna and I followed our routine and watched the weekly soap opera together (it was an evening soap opera that aired in prime time). We'd prop ourselves on pillows on my bed to watch the show each week, and we thought it was hilarious.

During one dramatic scene, we saw with glee that the backdrop of the set, which was supposedly a wall with a painting on it, wobbled along with the very dramatic lead actor, who was pounding his fist on a desk. With each pound, the set wobbled with equal drama. We were hysterical.

After the soap opera ended, Johanna went to her room and I began to read. It was very late, and there was still no sign of Frank. I felt a stirring of apprehension and began to watch the clock. At 2:00 a.m. I began to worry. I couldn't sleep, so I got up, made tea, and sat on the balcony where I could see the winding drive that came up the hill to our building. There was almost no traffic on the street. Another hour went by.

Johanna appeared at the balcony and asked if everything was all right, and I said no, that I was worried. She joined me with a cup of tea and we both set our eyes on the road. When I thought about the Venezuelan police, I didn't even want to imagine how they would treat someone like Frank. I was beyond grateful that Johanna could understand my situation. It was such a comfort. She asked me if I knew where he was that night or whom he was meeting, if I had any reason to be particularly concerned about this evening. I told her that I knew he was always on high alert about possibly being followed by the KGB. We fell silent.

I didn't know whether I should call Frank's case officer at home; I didn't want to disturb him until at least dawn. Johanna asked about the protocol. I told her there were code words we were supposed to use in these situations. She urged me to do so, but I waited until the sky became light. When I checked our address book, I saw that Frank had never written the number there. It was probably under a code name I had forgotten. I called information and to my surprise, the number was listed.

I called and his sleepy voice answered. Riddled with adrenaline, I cryptically tried to explain who I was by using Frank's code name. It was instantly obvious that he had no idea who I was and didn't know the code name. I couldn't chance saying anything more in case the phones were tapped. I said I would call him later at the office. "Hmm . . ." he said.

It was time for Johanna to catch the bus to school and I insisted that she get on it. I wanted things to look as "normal" as possible. Johanna wanted to stay home, but I argued with her. She said it wasn't fair to expect her to act normal and go through a whole day at school knowing her dad was missing and not being able to talk about it with anyone. I promised that I would call the school under whatever pretense, to alert her with any update. She reluctantly agreed, fighting yawns as she rushed out the door to get to the bus in time.

Not thirty minutes after Johanna left, I heard the private elevator kick into gear. It opened directly into our living room, so I stood in front of our door and waited. It stopped on our floor, the doors opened, and there was Frank. He was filled with remorse because he realized how frightened I must've been. He had been taking an antihistamine for allergy, which made him drowsy. When the agent left the room, he started making notes about the meeting and took the medication along with a drink. He then fell asleep. Through the night. Accidentally. He had no resistance to medication, but alcohol didn't help. I was furious.

I called the school and asked to speak to Johanna. They took her out of class and brought her to the phone in the principal's office. I said, "Daddy's home. He's okay. We'll talk later." I don't know what she told the principal about why she had to take the call.

I was relieved that the chief had been so baffled and so sleepy, and that my early morning call had made no sense to him. It also prompted me to realize that we should review the drill, so that he would be alert under whatever circumstances, should a real situation present itself. I thought about all the married women who only had to be worried about their husbands getting drunk and having sex with a wicked woman. Did they know how lucky they were?

End of School

By the time the school year ended, Johanna had made a lot of friends, most of them Venezuelans. She had starred in a play, been to the beaches, where she learned to dance barefoot on the sand to Latin rhythms, and traveled to Aruba on a senior trip. She told us that people away from the city were friendly and gracious and fun. I wish we had been able to make that discovery ourselves. When Johanna was voted as one of the princesses of the senior prom, we were delighted and proud. It was astonishing that she had come such a long way in such a short time. We were doubly proud when she graduated with honors.

Though Johanna enjoyed her teachers and had some great classes, the reputation of that school became badly besmirched by the rumor, then the proven fact, that an American male teacher had been luring young boys into a child pornography ring, the details of which I choose not to outline. Our friends' child was among the victims. This did not come to light until the summer after Johanna graduated.

More horror stories unfolded. There were security guards at the gate of this dilapidated school, and it surfaced that they had been dealing drugs to the students throughout the prior year. When I told Johanna about this, she shrugged as if that wasn't news at all.

Don't Tell Mama

Frank celebrated his fiftieth birthday without even a second look in the mirror to make sure he was still attractive. Under deep cover, early retirement was allowed and well deserved. There was no hint of a midlife crisis because the magic fifty made him eligible to retire, and on his birthday we hosted an intimate dinner at home, in the company of a couple who had become our best friends.

Now that he was planning on retirement from the CIA, we began to look into job offers that had been made in the past. In the meantime, Frank could make enquiries and stay in Venezuela until we made a change. The work he was doing there was prosaic and could be taken over by someone else without any complication. There was really no valid reason why he had been transferred here from Tokyo, but that was in the past.

When we were in the United States on home leave, Frank received a phone call from a friend in Hong Kong, offering him a very good executive position. It was with an American company and required experience in foreign countries, as the company was multinational. It was a great job, at more than twice the salary he was making, with perks we had never even dreamed of. The man who would be his immediate superior was a good friend whom we had met in Japan.

When Frank received the call, our three children were in the room. I was not. When he hung up, he joyously said, "I've been offered a great job in Asia!" John's immediate response was "Don't tell Mama."

Frank was like a man released from prison. He just couldn't stop beaming. It was providence that he would find a job so perfect for him and in such a short time.

The Tapestry Incident

We returned to Venezuela to go through the necessary formalities of Frank's resignation and, assuming there was no replacement for him by his cover company, to close the office. The president of the cover company had told Frank that he did not want to be involved with the CIA again under any circumstances, because he was so embarrassed and annoyed by the way they had interacted with him, or more to the point, the way they had *not* interacted with him. Frank's position ostensibly was more about public relations than contracts signed, and Frank had simply laid the groundwork for future business, so closing the Venezuela office did not constitute any great loss to the cover company. It worked out well for everyone.

When Frank advised the chief of station that he was going to retire from the CIA and resign from the cover company, the chief was quite perturbed. Even though he knew Frank had every right to give thirty days notice after twenty-five years under deep cover (including military service), he pressed Frank to stay because he was handling very sensitive agents. Frank felt no obligation, and explained that he had already lined up another job and had to fill it in a very short period of time. Shortly thereafter, Frank's cover company advised the Agency that it did not wish to continue their relationship.

Immediately, the Agency said they wanted to take over the office furniture, down to the last paper clip and ballpoint pen. That would be my job. I was to list every item that had been purchased, with receipts for everything.

This was a grinding job. Luckily, I did have all the receipts, but no matter how much detail it included, there was always something else they asked about. They were extremely annoyed that Frank was leaving, and every roadblock was put in our path.

It was a tense, unpleasant situation. Frank's contact from the embassy told him that this turn of events had made it necessary for him and his family to stay, when he had been hoping to be transferred. We certainly didn't blame him for that. He and Frank had an amicable relationship, and Frank had great respect for him, particularly his command of Spanish.

We were told an accountant would be coming from Washington to handle the turnover of the office furniture and equipment. They were "bringing in the feds," as Frank put it. The bean counter arrived. He was a walking cliché with his short-sleeved polyester shirt, thick glasses, and the requisite bad haircut. He checked off all the items on the list. Frank pointed out that the Peruvian tapestry was actually mine. That I had paid for it. They jumped at the opportunity to make a point, and said that everything in the office was theirs because it had been represented as an accoutrement to the office. Even though I had my personal receipt for the purchase of the tapestry, it was pointed out that my signature was on many of the purchases. They stayed firm. When Frank told me about this, I burst into tears and raged against this act of meanness. Did it seem fitting that we should leave with such animosity hanging between them? I suppose so. I could not stop weeping. We sat on the terrace with The Noise and drank large vodkas without talking.

What a guy.

The realty company handling the rent of our apartment allowed us to provide sixty days notice. The CIA told us they required ninety days notice. It was a thoughtless oversight on my part, as all previous rental agreements asked for thirty days. I had paid little attention to the fine print, not having foreseen the possibility of our leaving the apartment before our two-year lease was up. Usually the cover company would have been responsible for this, but because of our botched visa applications, the Agency had paid nine thousand dollars under our name, and therefore they said it was our responsibility. They were very upset with Frank's "abrupt" resignation and this behavior underlined it.

When Frank told the president of his cover company what was happening, he became very angry. "These people have been using our firm name down there, and I am honestly embarrassed at how we have been presented. . . . First they put you in a cheap hotel, and now they imply that the company didn't pay your rent? I'll never deal with them again."

The irony is that any cover company pays the expenses of their CIA employee, thus showing authenticity of the job. However, the CIA is supposed to reimburse this money. A CIA deep cover employee is free, even though he does a superb job.

My relationship with our apartment realtor had always been cordial. I suggested to him that an apartment as beautiful as ours, with a stunning view, would likely be snapped up, and if that were the case, we hoped it would be possible to reimburse us some of the money. He agreed.

Frank had one more meeting with an agent. The next day we would move to the hotel for a week. All of our linens, dishes, and clothing had been packed. I was very tired and depressed, and definitely drinking too much. I went to bed early. When I got up for my last morning in the apartment, I walked down the hall to the kitchen and there, propped against the wall next to our private elevator door in the living room, was my tapestry, all rolled up. The wooden strip on which it hung was cracked, indicating that Frank had ripped it from the wall.

The CIA had paid for the purchase of our tiny car, which was about as glamorous as the car we had in Tokyo. Since it was in our name, we were asked to sell it and turn the sale money in.

This little car had an impressive history through the span of our ownership. Little by little, pieces of it had disappeared while it sat in parking lots or on the streets. First the rear view mirrors were taken, then the antenna. Even the black rubber strips along the side of the car had been stolen. Once, the car broke down. We were near a tollbooth, so Frank was able to call a tow truck. When the truck came, the driver was about to hook the car to the truck when he pointed out that we had no bumper. We couldn't believe it. We were not in the habit of looking to see if we had a bumper before backing the car out of the garage.

This was the little jewel we were now supposed to sell. We took the first offer from a used car lot without argument. The used car salesman looked at us strangely as Frank and I smiled at each other lovingly, and hailed a cab.

No Gold Watch

We never did recoup our rental money. We asked our friends, the British couple who lived in our apartment building, to keep an eye out and see if the apartment was being rented. They wrote me and told me that there had been no apparent effort to rent the apartment. The three months of paid rent allowed them to redecorate, since it came furnished. The apartment was never shown.

We spent our last week in a beautiful hotel. The one without a kitchen. The cover company insisted that we be allowed these privileges. We had cocktails before dinner and ate in the restaurant like the other guests. Soon we would be over the prison wall, government permits in hand, and $100 cash for the policeman on the way to the airport. The first three months of Frank's retirement pension was withheld, representing the nine thousand dollars in rent.

Frank's retirement from the Central Intelligence Agency was ignored. There was no party. No gold watch. No acknowledgement of a job well done. No letter from Washington. No handshake. And no goodbye.

During the first of the next two gypsy years, when Frank and I were traveling alone and living for long periods of time in hotels, I would call the hotel manager immediately and ask for a refrigerator in our room. Then I would find a grocery store and stock the refrigerator with fruit and cheese and bread, as well as alcohol. I always had our heavy crystal highball glasses, so that we could have our drinks in the room, in our sweats, with our feet up. Even for the briefest time, we could make an attempt to feel at home. Not going out for dinner had become a luxury.

There are statistics regarding the most stressful situations suffered in a lifetime: the death of a spouse, a divorce, or a major move. I have a repetitive dream about the latter, which does not require the analysis of a therapist. The dream is that I am walking down a strange street, I'm lost and I have no money, no luggage, and no passport. It is a foreign place, but I know that my new home is somewhere behind a brick school house, but I cannot find the school, and I cannot speak the language. My terror awakes me. That dream still invades my sleep. Of course, the dream is related to the fact that I always looked for a home with easy access to the school. But I am still lost.

To this day, I am frightened about being lost, especially while driving. One wrong turn sends me into a panic, even though logic tells me that I can stop and refer to the map. My fear is visceral.

A Look Back

Nobody Knows Him

When a man is asked to pretend to be somebody he is not, it would be psychologically enticing to be someone more interesting than the person actually is. To be an international spy, pretending to be the sales manager of a mediocre business firm, is quite the opposite: it's making a huge subtraction from his self-esteem.

To be swaddled in the constrictive clothing of a man who doesn't necessarily have any imagination, any sense of adventure, or certainly any danger, is to make a substantial subtraction from his true worth. To truly be somebody who is in every way exciting, dramatic, and mysterious, and never be able to tell anyone but his wife, is a cruel fate. It is hard to live with, and hard to live without. The urge to drop just a hint was always there, particularly for deep cover people who wouldn't be doing it at all if they didn't have a large ego.

I think that this, and not the money, is the hardest cross to bear. Money doesn't mean anything to a man who is dazzling everyone around him just because of who he is. And what he is. And he is absolutely not a sales manager. We didn't know any one of Frank's colleagues in the CIA who had a cover job that would impress anybody. All the small victories are hidden. So hidden that Frank didn't know that there were victories, unless word was handed down to him from the embassy. Nor were there verbal kudos. It is understandable why these men drank too much. And became depressed. And frustrated. And tired. It was hard.

After several years with the CIA, and having worked with a number of agents, Frank remarked to me that although he admired his agents for the chances they took, and the danger they were willing to risk, his great disappointment was that all the foreign agents betrayed their country for one reason: money.

Frank was holding a drink, smoking a cigarette, and looking off into space when he brought this up. This was obviously something he had been thinking about for some time, and I could see that it really bothered him. He went on to say that not one of them mentioned the good of the free world, or a world without war, free of communism, or any other altruistic reason for what they did and the risks they took. Although Frank was usually younger than they were, they looked upon him as a father figure who would keep them safe, guide them, protect them . . . and pay them a lot of money.

When we were about to be transferred away from a country, the agents would always become fearful and lost, as though Frank was the only person who could be allowed to know of their deception. It did not appear that they felt shame or guilt. They simply needed Frank as a guardian angel to protect them. Ironically, it was almost as if he had indeed become a priest, listening to confession, absolving them.

Almost inevitably, each agent followed a ritual meeting with Frank. One might expect a very expensive bottle of scotch at every meeting, another would have personal requests, such as a particular golf club from the United States, material goods as well as money. For the most part, these agents were in high places in government, and would have copied sensitive documents to pass on to Frank, smuggled out in the form of microfilm placed in the false bottom of a thermos that Frank had provided. He had also provided the tiny camera to photograph documents without in any way being conspicuous. Their reward? It differed. In one case, Ashok's, it was the promise of the American government to get him out of his country to a job in the United States. This was an understandable request: his country was hell. But . . . he was still paid a lot of money.

On the day of our wedding, I entered the church and Frank, standing at the altar, looked at me, and then walked down the aisle toward me with his hand outstretched and tears in his eyes to claim me. I was bathed in the glow of Frank's admiration and pride. I was like a prize he had won. His approval was total. When this gift is bestowed, it must be honored. It was with this total approval and admiration that we brought up our children. Except for the few deliberate betrayals toward him, Frank was highly regarded in the CIA. He was entrusted with the most sensitive of cases. His agents trusted him. Money never proscribed fear . . . Frank reassured them. And his colleagues believed in him. He described his job to our son as being "one percent James Bond and ninety-nine percent Maxwell Smart."

"We're off on another adventure!" Frank would announce sunnily to the children as we took off, airborne, to God knows where. The future to him was always filled with promise, bound to be exciting. The children sometimes hated that expression, with father beaming and mother and offspring trying to hold back the tears as we made yet another move across the globe. But there were so many good memories of friendships cherished, some lost in passing, and all enriching, adding color to our lives.

The Children

Children are the innocent players in this game of espionage, not because of the nature of it but because it causes their lives to be uprooted, friends to be lost and left behind, and strange schools encountered. They might find themselves in cold or unwelcoming places where nobody speaks English. Sacrifices always have to be made in the lifestyle of a child. A bicycle must be stored because there is nowhere to ride it; there are no television shows or movies to watch, because they don't speak the language, and they can't even have the food they like to eat, because it isn't sold "there." And most difficult of all, the hardships involved in trying to make a new friend. Just one new friend.

How many times did I open a hotel room door to see my sweet Kristin, her head bowed, clutching her schoolbooks to her chest, her shoulders shaking with the sobs she was trying to stop, because she had her own little hell sitting in a room full of strangers, staying at her desk during recess staring at a book, rather than risk the school yard with its little cliques?

I sometimes wondered if it was worse in international schools, where friendships are coveted and clutched tightly, not to be interfered with by someone new, because experience had taught them that the friendship would last for only for a little while, and could not be shared. There is no largesse in the world of children. The world that remains stable for them is no larger than their parents and the familiarity of a few items of furniture like the dining room table, the sofa, the dishes, the clock, and the bed they knew from another country.

The lack of roots was an acute loss for me as well. In the countries we lived in, it seemed that other Americans had a home in California, or Georgia, or Texas, and that's where they would return. When sleep eluded and loneliness set in, they could draw an image of those places in their minds. Some were very lucky, and had an American home to go to during school vacations, so even when they came back three months later, they knew that it wasn't forever and the house waited for them.

Every time we moved, and the house hunting began, it was all about the children and the school and the doctor and the dentist, and were there any children their age in neighboring houses, and where did the school bus stop? At first I felt responsible for thrusting this life upon them, for Christmases with just the five of us and no extended family, for not having the opportunity to know their grandparents or aunts and uncles and cousins. And the sadness lay inside of me too.

And what about our boy John, who played soccer on the street with his Spanish friends, Lalo and Alejandro, who studied Spanish classical guitar and played the piano? John rushed into learning Beethoven. He and his father also played boogie-woogie together, sitting side by side on the piano bench. Once John played at a piano recital for children. Everyone else played little marches, and then John came and sat on the piano bench, and tenderly approached "Moonlight Sonata," playing it faultlessly to a hushed room.

One day John's sixth grade teacher in India called and asked me to meet her at the school. She told me that she loved this "engaging boy." She showed me a questionnaire that the children had completed, which asked, "Who do you want to be like when you are grown up?" John had written, "My father." After reading that, his teacher had asked him, "and what is your father like?" John replied, "I don't know." He had been separated from his father for six months before coming to this strange country, and his father had drifted into the mire of business.

I went straight from the school to Frank's office. I knew he would want to know. He was dictating to his secretary when I arrived, and I said I had to interrupt because it was important. Frank's eyes were brimming when I told him about the visit to the school. He said he would be home before John was, and they would spend time together.

Our youngest child, Johanna, was the one who seemed to have fewer heartaches, perhaps because her first foreign country, Spain, was actually her native land. In India, our driver's daughter became her best friend and they played games together in the garden. This child had a bravado that was entirely her own, under many circumstances. She left a foreign country by herself to go to college where her sister was, and she toured the campus on a bicycle, needing no guide.

Feeling like Exiles

On home leave visits to the States, we were almost always lucky enough to rent a furnished, private home for a month. Our good friends investigated all the possibilities and always found a house with a pool or near a beach. We wanted to be surrounded by our friends, and it was a wonderful way to do it, gathering around a pool. For a month, life became a veritable picnic. The kitchen was open house for food and drink, and the bar never closed. Our place was the center and we were catalysts who brought together a group who generally hadn't mingled for a year. They brought their children, their friends, and current wives.

These were friends we had known since our youth. We caught up on the latest happenings and the juiciest gossip. We could pick up where we had left off the previous summer. They were our dear pals forever. But we had changed and I think we had become different people. This was especially the case during our time in India. It had nothing to do with our friends, but it had everything to do with us.

We saw the world through different lenses and we didn't talk much about our life unless we were sharing an amusing story. In the sunlit ambience of a beautiful day in California, holding a glass of chilled Chardonnay, we were more than a world away. We had left the darkness. My stack of photographs of saris, bodyguards, and elephants remained in my handbag after the repeated experience of having friends absently shuffle through them while talking about something else. I could identify with this, remembering the shudder I felt when an airplane seatmate had reached into his briefcase and withdrawn a stack of pictures. I thought, dear God, please don't let these be pictures of unattractive children.

We learned never to begin to describe our life, even though it was just a vignette. Our experiences had broadened us, and the narrowness of interest we encountered was something we learned to expect and accept. We were foreigners. We had never anticipated how strange we would feel when we came home to visit or later, to stay. There was a sameness about everyone and from within these boundaries, we felt a restriction of communication that was disappointing. We felt like exiles.

The exceptions were people who at one time had lived overseas for a period of time. Almost immediately, we rushed into an exchange of stories with those people, and the feeling of being understood was mutual. These were our people. Conversely, there were times when we encountered people who had travelled to our foreign country on a vacation. Their own expert reactions were offered as lessons, just in case we had missed anything. "Professional travelers," we called them.

Even to this day, whenever there is a reunion with friends

we knew in a foreign country, there is a soul-mate flavor to our renewed alliance. There is also the shared and discussed experience of culture shock we've all encountered when coming home. This reaction applies when introduced to new friends who had also been nomads like us. With these people, there's always a rush of social exchange, with a sense of urgency about it. These people knew what it was like to change the way we had changed. We recognized each other. We were validated.

A Canadian man we knew had been a prisoner of war in Japan for five years, during World War II. Every year, those who survived had a reunion in a different city in Canada. How could anyone else ever know what was in their hearts with their shared experiences of nightmares and panic attacks, and the understanding of why they had become who they were as the years passed? Their fellow-survivors became their family, as their own brothers and sisters could never be. The bond of their pain shared and love given remained unique. Our experience, of course, could not in any way parallel or compare with the intensity of that experience, but the recognition is the same. I asked this Canadian man to come to visit us in Japan. "I was there once," he said, "and I didn't like it."

I Remember . . .

I remember a skiing trip to a place in Austria, accompanied by an American couple who lived in Madrid when we did. We were in the beginners class, from which I never graduated. The taut and tanned instructor spoke only German, which was understood by a Japanese girl in our class who translated it into Spanish for us. By the time we understood it, small children were catapulting by without poles, and we were careening all over the place in all directions. When we returned to the inn where we had adjoining rooms, we could hear the showers start, and the yelps and groans of our pain mingling when the water hit our bodies.

When we went to the dining room for dinner, Frank, proud of his college German, gave the order to the waitress, who covered her mouth to hide her mirth, and as the swinging door to the kitchen closed, we could hear shrieks of laughter. It seemed that Frank had ordered "a cold bird and a hot banana."

I remember our trip to Paris, where it rained and rained. It was as gray as our grief was at that time, having lost a very dear friend, and we went to Notre Dame Cathedral and lit a candle for him. On our first night, we found we were lost on what seemed to be a street of bars or cafés without dining rooms. We stopped in a bar and asked the bartender for directions. He apparently was the owner, about to close and make his dinner in living quarters behind the bar. He invited us to join him. His manner was brusque, but his hospitality was warm, as though thinking, "These people are Americans, so I had better not disappoint them by being charming." I think that being rude to Americans is the law in France. We sat in a back booth in candlelight, and though our communication was fractured, the meal was exquisite. Our host waved away our offer to pay . . . brusquely, as required.

I remember with particular delight standing in the middle of a main road during a fierce blizzard in Seoul, Korea. In truth, I was ankle-deep in snow, waving currency to entice anyone to drive me and my raucous Australian friend, Sheila, to the airport, because the taxis had disappeared with the wild weather. Sheila and I were on a buying trip, slipping and sliding through the back alleys of Seoul, looking for antique chests and dodging the kimchi breath of the local denizens.

I remember being on the island of Saipan and finding that

the manager of our hotel was a man who had worked in a hotel in India; we had known him socially. He joined us when we came down for brunch, and when I noticed there were no scrambled eggs in the chafing dish at the buffet, he stood up and said, "I'll go to the kitchen and make some more." When I seemed stunned, he said in his German accent, "The whole staff is drunk. They got paid yesterday." A local custom, he explained. That afternoon, he showed us what was left of a prisoner of war camp, pointing out an enclosure where it was said that Amelia Earhart had been held, and then he showed us the cliff where entire Japanese families had committed suicide standing in line, men, women, and children. Suicide was better than the shame of defeat. It was said that the women threw the children over the cliff first, so that they would not falter.

I remember crossing Switzerland by train from Milan. We didn't know it would take hours, and after three or four hours had passed, Frank staring out the window, glumly said, "I can't take much more of this relentless beauty." When we arrived in Geneva, we discovered that our hotel was in the red light district, and I was fascinated by the nocturnal transactions taking place on the street below our window. The Swiss had a red light district?!

I remember a place called Gulmarg. It is thirty miles from China, north of Kashmir. We took a plane, then a bus, then mules, and then sleds to reach a place that I considered to be the most beautiful place in the world. On New Year's Eve, having left the group drinking brandy around the fireplace in the lodge, I was on a path in the deep snow, going to our cottage. The snow hushed everything and the stars had multiplied into billions, so close and so clear that I could touch them. There was a woodstove in the middle of our small house where all five of us slept, and at times during the night, a sherpa would come in quietly and stoke the fire. At dawn he made tea in a kettle and put it on the stove for breakfast.

I remember a bullfight in Spain in early summer. We stayed in a small pueblo called Aranjuez, eating lunch outdoors, protected from the hot sun by huge, leafy trees, tasting the new asparagus and fresh strawberries, then walking to the plaza to see matador Palomo Linares. We would never have believed the passion around this dusty drama of the *corrida*, but everyone was smitten with the valor of this sixteen-year-old boy. After the bullfight, we went to a crowded bar, where Jack Palance asked me how to say vodka in Spanish.

I remember a cocktail party on a junk in the harbor of Hong Kong, at dusk, with a group of Chinese friends and a couple of British policemen. As we watched the lights of the city far away, I heard someone singing a Stevie Wonder song, made more haunting because it was sung with a Chinese accent. "I Just Called to Say I Love You."

I remember Easter in Venice, when the grumpy gondolier didn't sing, so I sang "O Solo Mio." Loudly. I was amazed that our children were not embarrassed. They laughed. I remember walking through the ruins of Pompeii with our children, after which John said, "It looks just like any old pueblo in Spain to me."

I remember going to the book fair in Frankfurt in winter. We stayed in Wiesbaden at the Rose Hotel. While Frank was at the book fair, I took a nap on a dark afternoon, covered by the most billowing comforter in Europe. It was snowing when I woke up, and I sent for tea and cookies.

I remember five days in London, getting away from Madrid, hungry for English movies and theater. Walking down Regent Street, looking for sales on cashmere sweaters, we commented that nobody on the street looked British. We made bets, and on the pretext of asking directions, I approached various people, but none of them was English. When we returned to the Hyde Park Hotel, we saw an Arab getting into a white Rolls Royce, and we agreed that we had finally found our first Englishman after we heard his chauffeur speak.

I remember the procession in Madrid on Good Friday. We were on a balcony overlooking the street. Leading the procession was a man carrying a life-size cross, as Jesus had. This parade had begun in the early morning, people walking on cobblestone streets, their feet bare. We saw the end of it at dusk, and their feet were bleeding. The cross was a heavy burden. The people lining the streets held lit white candles. Their sadness was made vivid by their total silence.

I have been shaped by these experiences, touched by the voices and the people and the places and the sounds and the smells. We had been making our own memories. It wasn't boring.

Post-CIA (1982-1986)

Legitimacy

Frank was excited about his first job after retiring from the CIA. We spent a brief time in the city of the corporate head-quarters of the firm Frank was going to work for. After we had been there for about a week, the president of the company and his wife invited us to dinner at their country club. We knew the club was exclusive when we arrived and saw the creaky, eighty-year-old waiters, all of whom knew our host personally. Inviting us there was a grand gesture not accorded to many. The personnel director, who had extended this invitation on the president's behalf, said she was dumbfounded. Nobody was invited to his club. We were impressed, but also puzzled. Our hosts showed a great interest in our experiences overseas. They were a gracious couple.

A few days later, Frank was called to the president's office for a chat. This is what the president shared with him. It seemed that the CIA had sent a man from Washington specifically to inform the president that Frank had been an intelligence officer with the CIA. This had been done with the obvious intent of hurting Frank's opportunity for employment with them, and supposedly to demonstrate to Frank that one does not leave the CIA when it is inconvenient for them. It was a cruel act of revenge and a calculated move, incurring the expense of a trip from Washington and hotel expenses. This was great largesse on the part of an Agency that heretofore couldn't reimburse us the cost of a shoeshine. In the past, whenever Frank had made trips to Washington, he always dealt with the same man who, he thought, acted in Frank's best interests. This was the man who had just visited the president of the corporation. This was a personal vendetta on the part of the CIA. As much as we had been maligned over the years, we would never have believed they would go this far.

As it turned out, the president of this company had already known about Frank's past, considering it one of the positive reasons for hiring him. Not a hindrance, but a benefit. What could be better, in the world of public relations and sales, than a smooth operator from the world of espionage? The pettiness of such a visit from the CIA was what prompted the president to invite us to dinner at his club. He not only was disgusted at the intent of this visit, he embellished on his good will with that very special invitation.

Frank had loved working for the CIA and was proud of what he had accomplished. In the years that followed his retirement, he missed the choreography of his days and nights and weeks, the surprises, the intrigue, the game. That game he had played for so many years was a source of pride, because he had always been one of the good guys.

He came to also love his new job. He was so accustomed to holding two jobs that he poured such zeal, and so much time, into his work that he became a boy wonder. I could buy a new dress and put away the tired dress that I had worn everywhere for so many years.

We were legitimate.

The New Real Job

The first three years of our life "uncovered" were spent in a tropical country. Frank's new job required him to deal with four different countries adjacent to our home base. He was thrilled with all aspects of his new position. It seemed tailor-made for his experience and style. It also made it necessary for him to be away from home almost all the time, so I stayed at home and watched the orchids grow. Frank's life was hectic, constantly in the fast lane he so loved, and the challenge to succeed was a joy to him. He did so well that he was promoted to a very responsible executive position at the home office in the heartland of America. He tried to refuse the position, but it was thrust upon him.

Finally we were living in America again and we bought our first house after twenty-seven years of marriage. It was a house with a huge kitchen with a fireplace in the middle, and wall-to-wall windows overlooking a huge patio where rabbits liked to visit. We were in a neighborhood where the elite enjoyed the good life, and our address was our calling card.

In Memoriam

One Saturday in late fall, crisp and shining, ablaze with the colors of Thanksgiving, we planned a lazy day: a trip to the library and a stop at the video shop to rent a movie. Frank was quiet and pensive. He asked me to drive, and that was unusual, but he said he was tired. And he looked tired. He had just returned from a long trip through Europe, and was, I thought, jet-lagged. He stayed in the car while I parked at the video store, telling me to choose the movie, as well as a book for him at the library. Walking away from the car, I turned and saw him standing, arms crossed atop the open passenger door, looking at me with a look so plaintive and so sad that I stopped for a moment. He waved with just a small gesture of his hand.

When we got home, I sat in the kitchen, leafing through my book, when Frank walked in and said, "I feel strange. I just feel strange." He looked pale and bewildered. I suggested he lie down so I could rub his back. He lay down on the bed, and I could feel that his breathing was ragged. Then he was overcome with a rattling that I could feel under my hands. "Hurts," he whispered. And then the sound and the trembling stopped. I ran from the room to find the cordless phone to call an ambulance, calling to Frank not to leave me, please not to leave me, in spite of my sure knowledge that he already had. He had led two lives. He had just turned 54 and it was time for his heart to stop.

⌀

The video I had rented was *The Trip to Bountiful*. It was about a woman who made a long and tortuous journey to return to her roots. When she got to her destination, it was just an empty house.